THE MERCHANT'S
PROLOGUE AND TALE

The Old Man and the Young Wife (see p. vi)

THE
MERCHANT'S PROLOGUE
AND TALE

FROM THE CANTERBURY TALES
BY
GEOFFREY CHAUCER

*Edited with Introduction, Notes
and Glossary by*
MAURICE HUSSEY

CAMBRIDGE
UNIVERSITY PRESS

Published by the Press Syndicate of the University of Cambridge
The Pitt Building, Trumpington Street, Cambridge CB2 IRP
40 West 20th Street, New York, NY 10011–4211, USA
10 Stamford Road, Oakleigh, Melbourne 3166, Australia

© Cambridge University Press 1966

Library of Congress catalogue card number 65-10545

ISBN 0 521 04631 9

First published 1966
Reprinted six times
Reprinted with new appendix 1975
Thirteenth printing 1996

Printed in Great Britain at the
University Press, Cambridge

CONTENTS

Frontispiece

Acknowledgements   *page* vi

Introduction   1

Text

  THE MERCHANT'S PROLOGUE   37

  THE MERCHANT'S TALE   39

  THE MERCHANT'S EPILOGUE   76

  PORTRAIT OF THE MERCHANT FROM
    THE GENERAL PROLOGUE   77

Notes   78

Appendix   103

Glossary   104

FOR
GODFREY HARRISON

ACKNOWLEDGEMENTS

It is a pleasure to thank the officers and staff of the Cambridge University Press for their careful assistance in the production of this volume.

For the reproduction of the Frontispiece I have to thank the Trustees of the British Museum. It is a print by one of two Westphalian artists bearing the same name, Israel von Meckenen. They were father and son and worked in the latter part of the fifteenth century and the early years of the sixteenth: there is no certain method of distinguishing their closely allied techniques. It will be agreed that the scene is an admirable realization of Januarie and May. They are seasonal symbols, as in the poem, and express personal desires equally appropriate to the Tale.

For this new impression I have revised some of the Notes and would like to thank my colleague, Mr James Winny, and Dr P. M. Vermeer for their suggestions. The portrait of the Merchant from *The General Prologue* has been added to p. 77.

M.P.H.

Cambridge
March 1968

A new appendix, on astronomical influences, was included in 1975.

INTRODUCTION

It has become an axiom in the criticism of Chaucer's Tales that the teller himself shall be implicit in the tale he tells, and that the two shall be interdependent. Thus, the reader's question will be: do the Prologue and Tale of the Pardoner, the Wife of Bath or the Merchant advance and develop the understanding of these characters already outlined in the *General Prologue*? In the case of the Merchant we are asked to account for the taste of cynicism that pervades the discussion of a serious topic—marriage—on which Chaucer wrote well and often. It might be thought that this is the result of the poet's own changing outlook; or it might, on the other hand, be an attitude, dramatically attributed to a fictional character, erected temporarily for the purpose of debate, and held to be inadequate. It would then be permissible to ask: is such cynicism a mature attitude? These are the points along which we may ourselves feel and develop with the poet; the best way to start seems to be with the first impressions that Chaucer has given us about the narrator who moves into the limelight to tell this story.

THE MERCHANT

In the *General Prologue* the portrait of the Merchant is unflattering. From it we draw a few well-known phrases:

> His resons he spak ful solempnely,
> Sowninge alwey th'encrees of his winning.

In modern terms this is a bore who insists on discussing his shrewd business deals all through dinner. He also has

I

a vested interest in the freedom of the seas—which makes him even worse—because he has a great deal of traffic on shipboard all the time. Chaucer makes him something of a hypocrite:

> Ther wiste no wight that he was in dette.

Yet being in debt is often the case of an investor, and in modern terms, again, there is provision for such contingencies in the bank overdraft. When Chaucer delivers his concluding snub it is a calculated affront and shows that the portrait is heavily charged with contempt:

> I noot how men him calle.

Most of the pilgrims remain anonymous, but they are not brushed off in this manner. It may be hazarded that Chaucer had his own reasons for disliking the recent operations of the merchant class in his own society. For whatever reason, the Merchant emerges from it as a secretive money-grubber, without attractive qualities.

From being a mere pilgrim each character in turn is built up into a narrator. The pilgrims have all just heard the Clerk's story of the supernaturally patient wife Grisilde as part of the marriage debate when the Merchant suddenly breaks the silence. He loses his original shyness and confesses that he has recently married a woman entirely unlike Grisilde. She is a source of weeping and wailing and it is because he is so disturbed by his reflexions that he now breaks out. Since such abruptness is unexpected, the onset of emotion which causes it is intended as a mark of self-revelation. He is a man of undetermined middle age, and now a disillusioned one. His story is of a man of sixty who wards off disillusion by complete failure to understand what is happening to his marriage. Very recently wed and quickly cuckolded, the protagonist Januarie is in a position hardly preferable to that of the unhappy Merchant himself. It is impossible to say whether or not the Merchant raises some of these issues because he feels the danger of being deceived in the same way, but something like this would explain the weight of masculine emotion in his narrative. He says as he concludes his Prologue that he will not indulge the company any more with his own 'soory herte', but instead he provides them with pages of love, hate, fear, sickness and misery, all made more bitter by an underlying irony which makes the listener squirm, since it is told with such art. Not, we say, Chaucer's own view: rather the narrator's own emotional pressure gives this Tale its doom-laden strength.

'THE CLERK'S TALE' AND
'THE MERCHANT'S TALE'

There is a distinct purpose in returning to the Tale that has just closed, if we are to see the architecture of the whole Canterbury Tales, enhancing with considered plan the value of the single part. The Clerk told of a Lombard count whose tenants, fearing the hazard of the future under an unmarried overlord, all petition him to marry and secure the future. Their wishes, expressed with dignity and conviction, find favour with him and dissuade him from his intent to remain a bachelor. His sober choice falls upon a country girl, Grisilde, whom he carries away to his palace and marries with suitable ceremony.

The resemblances and contrasts between this and *The Merchant's Tale* immediately strike the reader. Sir

Januarie is also a resident of Lombardy who suddenly decides in old age that he will marry, even though it is the task of one of his brothers to try to dissuade him. He finds the girl and his wedding is celebrated with splendid ceremony.

From this point the two tales diverge dramatically. To try her patience, Count Walter casts his wife off. He has her children taken away from her, and she submits to being sent back in disgrace to her native village. When Walter is satisfied with her reaction he sends for her again, ostensibly in order to assist at a feigned second wedding; and finally he restores her to her former position and love. The Merchant's narrative, on the other hand, shows the gradual dominance of the bride, who takes a lover and deceives her old husband until the end of the story. Both stories have a degree of allegory about them, but the Merchant's is a great deal more realistic in its handling of a grosser theme.

A further distinction which throws light upon the second narrative is in the difference between the two Lombardys. In the first the background is bleak and austere, conveying the impression of a time before Chaucer; whereas in the second there is a much finer and more colourful society, prefiguring the world of the Italian Renaissance. We might legitimately think of Januarie on a Florentine estate or in a Venetian palazzo if we are familiar with these images of magnificence.

It is possibly as a tribute to his Italian colleagues that the Merchant hints at a populous town in festivity:

> Al ful of joye and blisse is the paleys,
> And ful of instrumentz and of vitaille,
> The mooste deyntevous of al Itaille. (500–2)

The god Bacchus himself serves the drinks, and Venus too is present, as in a Renaissance painting. Yet in this culture, with its pagan leanings, the Christian religion is neither minimized nor satirized. The priest remains on hand right through the ceremonies and until the blessing of the bridal bed. He returns for the High Mass which is sung on the fourth day to greet the bride on her return to the Great Hall.

Yet, in spite of this, we are forced to accept a certain depravity in Januarie, the master of so much genuine splendour. It is strong enough to make nonsense of all the pretensions of his society, even though he is not typical of their way of life. He is both late and irregular in his manner of marriage, and while every lord will have a Placebo to echo him and act the role of the flattering sycophant, Januarie also has Justinus, who in lines 447–76 'places' and judges the whole affair, even if he is not permitted to influence the hero's decision. The world of Pavia contains the seeds of corruption even if it also has the makings of a successful life. After all, wealth was to be the making of the Medici family even if it hastened the fall of the Borgias. The distance between Pavia and London was enough to lend enchantment; for the benefit of the poem's completeness, the 'logic of the poem' as T. S. Eliot might have called it, the world is there: actions do not take place in a vacuum.

COURTLY LOVE

Readers of C. S. Lewis's celebrated *The Allegory of Love* will realize how closely *The Merchant's Tale* follows the fourfold conditions of medieval romantic love: Humility,

Courtesy, Adultery and the Religion of Love. The
Humility of Damyan before his master and his lady is
plain at his first appearance, but it wears off within the
time-span of the story (possibly a year). Courtesy is to be
found in the enlightened world of the poem and Adultery
made most plain in the first introduction of the lover, at
the very wedding-feast of his master. The Religion of Love,
a perversion of religion, prescribes a certain ritual in which
the lover is in pain in his search for recognition and
miraculously cured once it has been noticed.

A perfect guide to this Lombard triangle is to be found
in *The Art of Courtly Love* by Andreas Capellanus, not to
be confused with Martianus Capella, known as Marcian,
author of the book mentioned in lines 521-2:

> that ilke wedding murie
> Of hire Philologie and him Mercurie.

Marcian's is a heavily abstract work, where Andreas'—
which we cannot presume that Chaucer had read—is quite
blunt and operates from the proposition 'that one cannot
love one's wife, but must love the wife of another man'.
Andreas examines all the subsequent steps of romantic
entanglement which are the more exciting when for the
simpler delights of fornication the lover exchanges the
complicated ones of adultery. It has been shown that
C. S. Lewis was wrong to give the impression that all
courtly love stories are adulterous, since *The Franklin's
Tale* has for its opening premise a lover whose end is a
marriage of rare distinction. On the whole, though, the
state arose when wedded love, especially in those of high
rank, had nothing at all to do with romance. It was a
matter of dynastic arrangements linking two estates quite

as much as two individuals, enabling money to beget its percentages quite as easily as the couple did their children. Parents arranged the partners and the dowry often from the childhood of the participants, and all they had to do for their part was to live together. In a mansion this was relatively easy as there was some hope of escape. Love of this type in a cottage could only have been a purgatory.

As soon as the reader confronts *The Merchant's Tale* with a prior knowledge of the ideas and idioms of courtly love he notices a significant fact. The events and characters are so close to type that they have little individuality. She is the adored one who slowly comes round to requiting his love, and he is the adorer who has all the pangs of love-longing to undergo, and all the fears of discovery. He obeys all the rules of the game. His love-letter goes according to type. He is said to be 'gentil', 'servisable' and 'sike'. She, for her part, shows 'pitee and franchise' and she blesses him by bidding him to be 'al hool'. Then at once:

> Up riseth Damyan the nexte morwe;
> Al passed was his siknesse and his sorwe.
> He kembeth him, he preyneth him and piketh,
> He dooth al that his lady lust and liketh. (797–800)

He has felt the 'fyr', the 'desir' and the 'peyne' but she has shown her 'grace' and they have only to come to terms with their love and arrange the assignation. The vocabulary is as standard and commonplace as the situation itself and Chaucer has no emotion of his own to add to it. It is true that we would prefer to see her married to Damyan, yet she has accepted the contract to Januarie. Seeing the one in his 'sherte' must make her long to see the other instead, but the end of the story offers no

7

solution. She indeed has her lover, though he is no longer a 'servant'. He is exposed as rapacious and lustful, capable of giving her a short-lived passionate experience and quite as likely to abandon her. Even though the narrator expresses the deepest cynicism towards the marriage he has described in such intense detail he is equally disenchanted by the alternative. There is yet hope for a type of marriage which is outside his experience, and which is to be described in *The Franklin's Tale*.

THE GARDEN OF LOVE

One of the central images of the courtly romance is that of the love garden. It is therefore in accordance with the conventions that Januarie should lay out a garden near his home, a *locus amoenus* (a pleasant place) as it was called.

It is to the well-known *Roman de la Rose* by Guillaume de Loris and Jean de Meun that the Merchant directs us in a reference at line 820, but there are many other related works of European literature that Chaucer and his audience may have known. The earliest that remains is *Le Fablel dou Dieu d'Amors* ('The Fable of the God of Love') in which the ingredients are a garden, a stream, the god of love and the birds congregating to look for mates. In this example there is not only a lock and key but a drawbridge to exclude those who are not wanted. An example of this tradition which we know that Chaucer read was Boccaccio's *Teseide*, the source of *The Knight's Tale*. In this love garden Venus and Cupid make their appearance, with Bacchus and Ceres in attendance. The languors of love are portrayed in allegory and the work conveys the authentic spirit of the courtly love vision. There

is also Chaucer's own *Parlement of Foules* in which the
traditional vision of a spring morning is held on St
Valentine's Day.

The Parlement is the poem to look at to gain a pleasing
view of the love vision. In it Chaucer is led into a garden
by the spirit of Scipio Africanus when he is too old for
romantic illusions himself (it is the year 1382):

> For thou of love hast lost thyn tast, I gesse,

says his guide. They look into the park at the vegetation,
the allegorical residents and the birds, and they pass
through gates with inscriptions in golden letters, telling
of the blisses of love, and others in black letters, which
contain threats:

> 'Thorgh me men gon,' than spak that other side,
> 'Unto the mortal strokes of the spere
> Of which Disdain and Daunger is the gyde.'

Love is composed of an equal draught of delight and
disdain, it is assumed, and to enter its world is to accept
both aspects. The inscription just quoted is reminiscent of
the words written over the portals of Hell and described
in Dante's *Inferno*, a visionary poem that Chaucer knew
well. In that work the inscription tells only of the dangers:

> Per me si va nella città dolente;
> Per me si va nell'eterno dolore;
> Per me si va tra la perduta gente.

(Through me is the way to the doleful city, is the way
into eternal pain, is the way among the people who are
lost.)

Through the more modest *wiket* of Januarie's garden
people go to find the adorable qualities of love that are

9

associated commonly with Venus. She had appeared at the wedding and has withdrawn. There is also mention of Priapus (the god of gardens and the god of orgiastic sexuality) and the presiding god is Pluto, whose rape of Proserpina is one of the greatest of all fertility and vegetation myths. The steady accent upon violence in this garden, as in the whole poem, is familiar enough to the modern reader. There has been Januarie's view of sex as violence inflicted upon the woman; Pluto and Damyan exploit the same characteristics towards their partners; there is a complementary lack of respect and deep affection all round. Thus the power of the scene in the Pavian love garden comes from its inversion of the traditional or conventional order of such things and its lack of refinement and elegance. Even the number of the occupants (three humans) is wrong, and its emphasis upon carnality instead of courtliness quickens the audience's appreciation of the corruptness of this trio.

Chaucer's final comment upon the melody and euphony of tradition comes in the gross image with which the whole story culminates:

> And sodeynly anon this Damyan
> Gan pullen up the smok, and in he throng. (1140–1)

After that there is no time for beholding the rose garden.

THE GARDEN OF EDEN

Even with all this before us, the image of the garden is not yet exhausted. The one interpretation of it that would spring first to the medieval mind has not yet been mentioned: the Garden of Eden in Genesis. This too is an allegory of the fall of love and the failure of humanity to respond to the opportunities of a Golden Age.

Januarie's walled garden was conceived as a locked paradise for a rich couple to roam about in. Adam and Eve were endowed with far more than earthly riches and their catastrophe was far more terrifying. In Genesis the judgement is expressed thus:

cursed is the ground for thy sake; in sorrow shalt thou eat of it all the days of thy life; thorns also and thistles shall it bring forth to thee; and thou shalt eat the herb of the field; in the sweat of thy face shalt thou eat bread, till thou return unto the ground; for out of it wast thou taken; for dust thou art, and unto dust shalt thou return. (Genesis iii)

Under Chaucer's precise control, *The Merchant's Tale* is full of menace, and irony pervades every serious issue. Quite early in the Tale Januarie's mind had strayed towards the original Paradise Garden:

> womman is for mannes helpe ywroght.
> The hie God, whan he hadde Adam maked,
> And saugh him al allone, bely-naked;
> God of his grete goodnesse seyde than,
> 'Lat us now make an helpe unto this man
> Lyk to himself'; and thanne He made him Eve.
>
> (112–17)

Unaware of the error of his ways, Januarie grows lyrical, singing of his lot:

> wif is mannes helpe and his confort;
> His paradis terrestre, and his disport.   (119–20)

The most trenchant comment on such a state of mind is available for a modern reader in Milton's *Paradise Lost*: a Hell rather than a Paradise with

> neither joy nor love, but fierce desire.

There is no better description of the reality of that paradise garden: the image stands up in the full horror of its traditional Christian meaning. Januarie and May have before them Damyan, the 'naddre' and 'scorpion', who is the scourge that they each deserve for their unworthiness in promoting neither joy nor love but yielding to fierce desire and calling it by a romantic name.

Other references to the Old Testament are both numerous and dramatic in *The Merchant's Tale*, a fact which illustrates the poet's understanding of the religious teaching of a Church he followed at a critical distance. A most simple example occurs in line 150:

> Lo, how that Jacob, as thise clerkes rede,
> By good conseil of his mooder Rebekke,
> Boond the kides skin aboute his nekke,
> For which his fadres benison he wan. (150–3)

The subject of the example is rather Rebecca than Jacob, since it is she who appears again in line 492. There is nothing creditable in her act of deceiving a blind man by presenting her smooth son Jacob as his hairy brother Esau. She is put forward nevertheless as an example of feminine resourcefulness; her inclusion is powerfully ambivalent. For the husband who is deceived the action can only be interpreted as a crime. On her second appearance Rebecca is cited together with Sara, who drove away her husband's concubine and illegitimate son in order to establish her own power. The humour of this reference is that it is derived from the marriage service, which seems to be sanctifying feminine deceit and making it a virtue. The Catholic nuptial mass at the present day still invokes their names: 'May she please her husband as did Rachel; be prudent, as was Rebecca; long-lived and faithful, like Sara.' One can hardly get married with such knowledge and fail to receive Chaucer's message.

In *The Wife of Bath's Prologue,* that lady's most recent husband, Jankyn, is a great student of the wiles and destructive tendencies of women. He reads example after example to his lady and forces her to swallow the insult to her sex. There is the same disillusion in the list of examples marshalled by the Merchant, although the emotion is hidden. Judith, cited in line 154, saved the Israelites, but only through the murderous cunning practised upon the life of Holofernes. Abigail presents another ambiguous situation since she contracted a marriage with David extremely soon after the death of her husband Nabal, whom the Lord conveniently smote, while Esther, whose case follows, saved her husband but killed Haman. All these excerpts might have come from Jankyn's book, that Bible for the misogynist, and presented images of danger and deception under the guise of admiration and appreciation.

The richest imagery from the Old Testament that remains to be analysed is to be found in the parody of The Song of Solomon used to welcome May into the walled garden. Januarie greets her in these lines:

> 'Ris up, my wif, my love, my lady free,
> The turtles vois is herd, my dowve sweete;
> The winter is goon with alle his reynes weete.
> Com forth now, with thine eyen columbin,
> How fairer been thy brestes than is wyn.
> The gardyn is enclosed al aboute.'   (926–31)

Our first reference is to chapter IV of The Song of Solomon:

> A garden inclosed is my sister, my spouse;
> a spring shut up, a fountain sealed.

It is a point that Chaucer does not explicitly make but it helps us interpret his other comments. The garden in the quotation from Solomon is a symbol of fertility and an image of all womankind. May and Januarie are keeping to the spirit of this text since the jealously guarded but cunningly duplicated key allows entry to both men at once. It is as Januarie expected—May is a Paradise in herself, but he had not foreseen the force in Justinus' premonition:

> Paraunter she may be youre purgatorie! (458)

The passage at the head of the last paragraph is a parody of verses from The Song of Solomon. In traditional commentary on the Bible the reference is to a mystical union of Christ and the Church, but in the Merchant's narrative there is only the physical world to portray. Solomon sings in the Old Testament in these words:

Rise up, my love, my fair one, and come away.
For lo, the winter is past, the rain is over and gone;
The flowers appear on the earth; the time of the singing
    of birds is come, and the voice of the turtle is heard in our land.

Doves, associated with Venus because of their promiscuity, are part of the Biblical imagery as well. Two religious cultures blend perfectly: when one is prepared to think solemnly of Christian love, one is confronted with the face of pagan lust as an alternative.

It has been pointed out that there is reminiscence in this scene of the sharply contrasted story of Susanna and the Elders, so familiar in the Middle Ages. Susanna, a beautiful woman, is, unlike May, a good and virtuous wife, who went into a private garden with her maids to bathe. The Elders are two lustful old men, not entirely different from

Januarie, who put an infamous proposition to her. They want her to yield to their senile lusts or in revenge they will swear to her husband that she is in the habit of admitting a young man to the private retreat. Susanna refuses outright and the Elders carry out their threat. The case is heard by Daniel who confounds the old men and has them summarily executed.

The image of Susanna's garden can carry this interpretation for its readers because, although it is an idealized world, it has a lock and key which are prominently displayed in medieval pictorial representations of it. Inside it there are the 'allees' to roam in and the 'laurer alwey grene' of *The Merchant's Tale*.

There remains in our imagination, high above our heads, the image of the tree, as powerful an image as any in the poem. It is at first the pear tree of medieval comedy and as such familiar to the original hearers. It is also the tree of the fruit of good and evil in which the serpent took up his abode. Again, it is an image of Januarie himself. Early in the poem he remarks:

> Though I be hoor, I fare as dooth a tree
> That blosmeth er that fruit ywoxen bee;
> And blosmy tree nis neither drye ne deed.
> I feele me nowhere hoor but on myn heed;
> Myn herte and alle my lymes been as grene
> As laurer thurgh the yeer is for to sene. (249–54)

He is mistaken; he is not an evergreen. He is not living through a midwinter spring, but through the onset of lasting winter itself. When he is taken towards the infamous pear tree he has not realized that every paradise must have such a source of evil. Because he is blind he does not see Damyan in the branches. He stands leaning against the trunk and bending slightly so that his wife can climb upon his back. He is shown, too, pathetically embracing the trunk of the tree as if to prevent anybody from following her up it. His jealousy has been aroused, but he does not realize his precautions are far too late and he is seen clinging to the instrument of his own ruin. He does not see the tree for what it is because he cannot see the evil in his own life. Once his sight returns he still remains blind to the evil he has promoted. The tree is a symbol of so much felt experience and so much complete lack of insight: it is a poet rather than a preacher who can make statements of such a degree of subtlety as this.

JANUARIE

Damyan and May have already been dismissed as stock types, perfectly fitted for the role of courtly lovers and without the slightest individuality of character. In this respect they throw into relief the only true creation of the Tale, its protagonist. It is quite wrong to reduce him to the abstraction 'Elde' (Old Age) since he is one of the poet's most complex characters.

It is from him that almost all the ironies of the poem originate. In M. H. Abrams's invaluable *Glossary of Literary Terms* (under 'Irony') the following is to be found:

To keep up a sustainedly ironic document, the writer is apt to utilize the device of a naive hero, or of a naive narrator or expositor, whose invincible obtuseness leads him to persist in putting an interpretation on affairs which the smiling reader just as persistently alters or reverses.

The Merchant's Tale has a subtle mind behind the narration, whether this is read as the Merchant or Chaucer himself. The rest of the quotation fits Januarie, the naive hero, to perfection. He is always unaware of the fullest implications of what he says. The long speech on marriage at the opening of the Tale is more appropriate in the mouth of the hero than of the narrator:

> And certeinly, as sooth as God is king,
> To take a wif it is a glorious thing,
> And namely whan a man is oold and hoor;
> Thanne is a wif the fruit of his tresor.
> Thanne sholde he take a yong wif and a feir.... (55-9)

If one stops at that point, there are already many ironies to explain. The first two lines are the declaration of his subject. It is not certain from the tone of the passage whether Januarie recognizes (as the readers do) that he is at that very moment 'oold and hoor'. The word 'fruit' refers the reader forward, all the way to the catastrophe in the pear tree, while the word 'tresor' brings into the poem the financial imagery, the economic motive which is found at every point in Januarie's view of marriage as a financial contract or an animal passion but as nothing of greater value. Ironies such as these run throughout the entire poem and reveal themselves in due order as the present moment sheds a light upon the false security of the past. These are images of return which are completely understood only when their full significance is revealed, but even before, they have enough potential to make the reader smile and flinch at once.

What is so subtle in the presentation of Januarie is the way in which our emotion flows out towards him because he is growing senile, is blinded and betrayed; yet quite as swiftly recoils because of his repulsiveness, his sheer profligacy and the hypocritical remarks he makes concerning the safety of his soul. The bedtime lectures that he gives to a deaf audience of one evoke universal contempt.

There is a great deal more to discuss, however, on the score of the quality Chaucer calls 'fantasye'. Januarie seems to believe that matrimony will make perversions into virtues. He is, as a result, perfectly accurate in his assessment of the possibilities of marriage without realizing that he has none of the qualities needed. This much being granted for a moment, it is natural for him to arrange everything as he does. He is fool enough to see himself as a rebirth of Paris ready to carry off a Helen, when he is more properly a fool of an old husband, a Menelaus, if ever there was one.

His insensitivity emerges in his belief that everything in life has a price ticket round its neck. As soon as he finds his wife he makes ready:

> every scrit and bond
> By which that she was feffed in his lond.   (485–6)

He does not pause to ask why there is no father to give his daughter a dowry. His creation of a pleasure garden is presented to us as an extension of a cashbox in which the key is the all-important possession.

Logically still, a man of his background sees sex as something to snatch, and all relations between the sexes as a kind of war:

> But in his herte he gan hire to *manace*
> That he that night in armes wolde hire *streyne*
> *Harder* than evere *Paris* dide *Eleyne*.   (540–2)

The Tale follows him still further but without pornography:

> Allas, I moot *trespace*
> To yow, my spouse, and yow greetly *offende*.   (616–17)

18

For a time he is so preoccupied with thoughts of his own potency that he does not see it as unnatural, since it has to be fed on a cupboard full of drugs and directed by the reading of a book entitled *De Coitu*.

All this is simple to analyse and to judge, but there is another side to him. His home and estate reflect the good taste of the day; his concern for his servant Damyan, ironic as it is, occupies many lines and is greeted by the rest of his household in terms that are completely unsmiling and unironic:

> And for that word him *blessed* every man,
> That of his *bountee* and his *gentillesse*
> He wolde so *conforten in siknesse*
> His squier. (704–7)

In the catastrophe of the poem we give him our pity again with his infamous wife crawling on his back to meet a scoundrel aloft in the pear tree. Pluto's sudden kindly action reveals May as she really is, though she is given what may truly be called infernal prompting to evade her husband's just wrath. It is the reader's judgement that the man of her own choice is younger but essentially no better. Damyan is likely to fasten upon her when she is a rich young widow until she (and he for that matter) must look elsewhere again for satisfaction.

All readers recognize the physical comedy of the bedroom scenes:

> And upright in his bed thanne sitteth he,
> And after that he sang ful loude and cleere,
> And kiste his wif. (632–4)

To use a modern image, the camera has come too close and seen the texture of the skin. In fairness to Januarie, though, it is a good and natural expression of his emotions to sing in such a situation in the dawn's first light; the reader is divided in his attitude.

Care and judgement have gone to the entire presentation of this man. There is no doubt that the reader feels a degree of projection of himself into him: empathy rather than a fellow feeling or full sympathy. He is a man who has not grown up. Although past sixty he still looks for one thing:

> He purtreyed in his herte and in his thoght
> Hir fresshe beautee and hir age tendre,
> Hir middel smal, hire armes longe and sklendre. (388–90)

He imagines that what attracts him is quite other:

> Hir wise governaunce, hir gentillesse,
> Hir wommanly beringe, and hire sadnesse. (391–2)

The lady of his hurried choice obeys the first canons of taste but never the second. It is all explained in the subtle image of the mirror:

> Many fair shap and many a fair visage
> Ther passeth thurgh his herte night by night,
> As whoso tooke a mirour, polisshed bright,
> And sette it in a commune market-place,
> Thanne sholde he se ful many a figure pace
> By his mirour. (368–73)

The language of psychology in these extracts is delicately handled: 'purtreyed in his herte', 'passeth thurgh his herte'; but there is no discrimination in a mirror, which is the symbol of his mind. Mirrors cannot reflect *gentillesse*, which for Chaucer is a Christian quality; they have no power to discriminate in the 'commune market-place' where, by implication, Januarie found May. He brings nemesis upon himself: good wives are not found in the market-place or the brothel. We are unlikely, since we all imagine ourselves basically decent, to sympathize; but we are ready to discuss sexual morality in the light of this vivid story. This is the best assent we can give to the creation of a satirist.

THE POETRY

Those who write about Chaucer are often accused of ignoring the native elements in his art and concentrating instead upon his handling of foreign models. The all-encompassing native element is, of course, the use of language; and the reader's wish is not to be deterred by the spelling or the syntax but to try to appreciate what he reads as he would a poem written in later centuries. The editions of Tales in this series aim to make this task lighter by reducing to a minimum the philological information and helping the reader with the task of critical appreciation.

The next four pages give examples which illustrate Chaucer's handling of English, a language which had not been in the widest public use when Chaucer began to use it. The treatment is not exhaustive, since it is far more helpful to the student to find further examples for himself.

Most considerations of Chaucer's style stem from the fact that his poetry was written to be read aloud and not perused silently in our own manner. Thus the pace of absorption would be slower and the attention more concentrated. The man with the book in front of him can turn back for purposes of clarification but if, as in broadcasting, the text is irrecoverable, the greatest virtue in its style is clarity, brevity and discipline. One of Chaucer's later disciples, the printer Caxton, wrote that the poet 'comprehended his matter in short, quick and high sentences, eschewing prolixity' which tells us what was thought a virtue in a poet in his own time.

Occasionally there must be relaxations of attention, passages in which the information-content is low. The effect on those occasions will be emotional and not narrative. Here is an example:

> O perilous fyr, that in the bedstraw bredeth;
> O famulier foo, that his service bedeth;
> O servant traitour, false hoomly hewe.   (571–3)

This passage is entirely of exclamation and many of Chaucer's tales can show pieces to parallel it. The device probably originated in the pulpit, which is very similar to the poet's lectern: each was designed for an artist in the spoken word. The third line in this passage says the same thing twice in different words so that the speed of comprehension is allowed to slow down, giving the audience a moment for breath before plunging ahead into the story.

When we encounter the rather pleasing songs that Januarie sings there seems no reason to think that the reciter did not sing them, since we know that singing during sermons was permitted. When the story reaches the idyllic moment in the garden and the verse grows lyrical the poet sings with Januarie:

> 'Ris up, my wif, my love, my lady free,
> The turtles vois is herd, my dowve sweete;
> The winter is goon with alle his reynes weete.' (926–8)

Similarly since there are six quite distinct characters who speak, the narration must have been a good deal more dramatic than we immediately imagine.

One of the most pregnant forms of oral expression is the proverb. This gives in the fewest possible words the greatest amount of moral wisdom. It is impossible to be dogmatic about what was a proverb and what was not at a distance of six hundred years, but we can say with some certainty that many phrases and lines have a proverbial ring about them. If they were already known they could act as a series of oases for the listener or monitoring stations from which the poem's progress can be judged. Their crispness of sound and movement correspond precisely with the qualities most admired by Caxton and they condition the audience as they are heard in turn. They also invite the reader to assent to a piece of wisdom which is shared by the whole folk.

What is noticeable about the proverbs in *The Merchant's Tale* is that they are occasionally inverted and used as a criticism of the speaker. Here is an example:

> 'Bet is,' quod he, 'a pyk than a pikerel,
> And bet than old boef is the tendre veel.'   (207–8)

In these analogies Januarie seeks to justify his marriage with a girl one-third of his age. But it turns marriage into a matter of physical eating, of greed; and is not Januarie 'old boef'? What has been called Chaucer's favourite line also has a proverbial ring to it:

> ...Pitee renneth soone in gentil herte.   (774)

True as this sentiment may be, it is once more restricted in application. It was intended for a nobler scene than the one in which May contrives her forthcoming adultery with Damyan.

Lines 620–1 and 627 may be consulted as further

23

proverbial influence, and there are many more which have the air of being on the way to a proverb:

> Paraunter she may be youre purgatorie! (458)

The final proverb in the Tale is another one inverted through its appearance in an ironical context:

> He that misconceyveth, he misdemeth. (1198)

May's words stand out as what we expect of folk-wisdom though the interpretation that we have to put upon them is more complex. Januarie has not misunderstood the message of his senses, but he has been led to doubt it by the persuasion of his wife. He accepts the conventional interpretation without causing further trouble.

The last quotation is an example of the parallelism which is occasionally employed in Chaucer's mature verse. There is a finality and elegance about the expression which is based upon the repetition of the syllable *mis*. The same technique is present in such a line as the second one here:

> And with this word this Justin and his brother
> Han take hir leve, and ech of hem of oother. (477–8)

It is only a short space from such a construction to a case of perfect antithesis which gives the sense of finish to the line and leaves it memorable and exact:

> Whan tendre youthe hath wedded stouping age. (526)

Anybody who is familiar with the couplet-technique of the eighteenth century will feel that Chaucer had discovered some of its secrets centuries before. What is even more felicitous about this quotation is that when Alexander Pope, the eighteenth-century poet, translated this Tale in

his youth under the title *January and May*, he had no need
to change the movement of this line, which emerges as:

> When tender youth has wedded stooping age.

A most useful exercise of comparative reading lies in this
version by Pope in imitation of Chaucer, a writer he very
much admired for a brevity, speed and moral vision so
like his own.

The handling of single lines as entities in themselves is
often sharp enough without the appendage of the second
line. Nowhere in the poem is there a better example than
the alliterative:

> Lo, where he sit, the lechour, in the tree   (1045)

which is brutally exposed and spotlighted as it should be.
How completely different is the love-movement which we
find in the following line and its echoes:

> He kisseth hire, and clippeth hire ful ofte.   (1201)

These are a few examples of the writer's sensitivity to
language and its qualities of immediacy and swiftness.
Nobody could ask for more perfect delineation of the
decrepit old man in bed than this:

> He lulleth hire, he kisseth hire ful ofte;
> With thikke brustles of his berd unsofte,
> Lyk to the skin of houndfissh, sharp as brere.
>
>   (611–13)

The verse does exactly what it says, it acts out the bristly
cheeks which are trying to be tender but are actually sharp
and repellent. Such is the range of the verse-movement
in *The Merchant's Tale*.

CHAUCER'S SOURCES

Chaucer assembled what we would nowadays call a working library of literature upon love and marriage. His selection contains works that are no longer at all widely read for their own sakes and none of those which are mentioned here has the same claims upon our attention as English sources. Prominent among his collection are Latin books: St Jerome, *Against Jovinianus*, used in *The Wife of Bath's Prologue*; Theophrastus, *The Golden Book of Marriage*; and *The Consolation of Philosophy* by Boethius to which Chaucer constantly refers. There are also two Latin works by Albertino: *The Love of God* and *Consolation*. None of these titles indicates a plot-source; each of them is philosophical, the source of sententious observations and epigrams. It has also been shown that Chaucer drew on his own two moral prose tales, *Melibeus* and *The Parson's Tale*, for the same purpose of strengthening the fibre of *The Merchant's Tale*. Admittedly, such identifications are slightly more problematical, and it may only be that he is returning to the sources of reflexions in those tales and not once again living off his old manuscripts.

There are three much more important sources to be mentioned since they lead back to the incidents in the narrative itself. It should be noted, however, that no source for the whole Tale has ever been found, only for single incidents. First of these is the situation of Januarie making up his mind to marry and consulting his friends for the purpose. Here the source identified is the poem *Mirror of Marriage* by the French poet Deschamps who was about six years Chaucer's junior and an acquaintance.

This is a long allegory whose scope is best understood from the following synopsis:

A man, of suitable age, feels the prompting of certain inner impulses towards marriage. These impulses induce a foolish, deceitful...line of reasoning, involving a form of mental slavery. He decides to inquire into all that can be learned about the subject of marriage. He then makes up a mental balance sheet, the headings of which might be respectively Impulse and Knowledge. After deliberation he decides to follow the latter.[1]

The reader sees the resemblance, but is even more impressed by the differences. The hero is *of suitable age* and he is swayed in the end by reason. Instead of two other voices to make the debate more clear and objective Deschamps provides five. These are the ingratiating sounds of Desir, Servitute, Faintise and the woman Folie on the one hand, and Repertoire des Sciences on the other. Professor McGalliard's study of the long poem shows that incidents occurring later in the Tale may be suggested in embryo by the French poem but the pattern of resemblance is not sufficient to revive an interest in the French writer's work.

The scene in which Januarie is bedded with May has for its source a long speech in the story *Ameto* by Boccaccio, one of Chaucer's most fruitful Italian sources. In the Italian original the speaker is Agapes the young wife. Her experiences are closely followed by those accorded by the English writer to his character, May. Where May is completely tacit, Agapes gives a full account of what she has suffered and reference to her comments will show that Chaucer exhibited delicacy and restraint in his treatment of this grotesque incident.

[1] J. C. McGalliard, 'Chaucer's *Merchant's Tale* and Deschamps' *Miroir de Mariage*', *Philological Quarterly*, xxv, 207–8.

The final episode, the tree-tryst, may be traced to a variety of sources, both oral and written. A version such as that known as *The Enchanted Pear Tree* was probably known to Chaucer. A more daring parallel exists in the legend that inspired the Cherry Tree Carol, one in which the husband Joseph (some legends say suspicious of his wife's mysterious pregnancy) has to satisfy the longing of Mary for cherries. A fresh dimension is added to the entire sequence if it is recalled that the pear has been held as a male sexual-symbol and that the passage gains a typically bitter-sweet flavour from Chaucer's ambivalent treatment of the entire Tale.

None of these sources covers much of the ground of the Tale; so the variety and pace of the story, together with much observed detail, can stand up as truly Chaucerian. The reader who wishes to discover all he can on the subject of Chaucer's sources is referred to the standard book on this topic in which the main works are set out in detail: Bryan and Dempster, *Sources and Analogues of 'The Canterbury Tales'*, pp. 333–56.

One other Latin work deserves separate treatment: Claudian's poem, *The Rape of Proserpina*, which is more than a source-book, almost a metaphor of the whole action. It is from this that Chaucer derived some of his information upon Pluto and Proserpina, although the legend was extant in other forms. In this poem, Pluto, the Lord of Erebus, is irritated because he has no wife. Because he lives underground he is cut off from the upper world and figuratively speaking blinded. Like Januarie, he too has brothers upon whom he calls, and these are the omnipotent Jove and Neptune who find him Proserpina for a bride. With Venus as intermediary Pluto is able to carry off Proserpina, although her mother Ceres had removed

her to Sicily for safety. The poem is unfinished but
includes a nuptial scene in which the bridal bed is blessed
by the hand of Night. Had it continued, the poem might
well have related that Proserpina was always anxious to
escape from her husband and succeeded in doing so for a
period of six months in every year. Chaucer places this
unhappy couple from the infernal regions beside the
subjects of his Tale, and indicates to readers by his
reference to the Latin writer that they might ponder the
juxtaposition.

What he does is to draw together the two worlds of
paganism and Christianity by giving Januarie and May
counterparts from a completely separate order of creation.
One of the couples acts as a symbol of the other and
broadens the application of the poem's principles. It is
the device that Pope later used in much more compressed
form. Maynard Mack has demonstrated that the classical
names used in Pope's poetry and the classical references
in the background of so many of his satires give a meta-
phorical colouring to the whole work. They may add the
tone of the mock-heroic, point out the central meaning of
the poem or control the reader's attitude to its moral.[1]
Chaucer's addition of Pluto and Proserpina puts the gods
in their places and defines the type of Hell that can be
lived by human beings who act blindly and selfishly.
Claudian is Chaucer's authority for these observations:

> In Claudian ye may the stories rede.   (1020)

Readers of Claudian in Chaucer's audience are able to take
this hint and study the metaphor.

[1] Maynard Mack, 'Wit and Poetry and Pope', *Eighteenth Century
English Literature*, ed. James L. Clifford (Oxford University Press).

2-2

'THE MERCHANT'S TALE' AND
'THE FRANKLIN'S TALE'

It has been remarked that *The Franklin's Tale*, the next but one in the series, is Chaucer's corrective for the taste left behind by *The Merchant's Tale*. There is indeed a marked resemblance between them, and one would not expect Chaucer to be guilty of repeating his message. In each tale a rich couple has a young man close at hand who offers to destroy their marriage. On the second occasion the husband is absent, not merely unaware of what is taking place, and he thus unwittingly leaves his wife to make the crucial decision. Again a garden is the *locus amoenus* of intended adultery:

> And craft of mannes hand so curiously
> Arrayed hadde this gardyn, trewely,
> That nevere was ther gardyn of swich prys,
> But if it were the verray paradis.

The lover, taking advantage of Dorigen's isolation, is subject to all the complaints of his class:

> In languor and in torment furyus
> Two yeer and moore lay wrecche Aurelius.

The reader also notices familiar terms: 'servant', 'servage', 'peyne', 'grace', 'torment'. This time, however, the lady Dorigen refuses to bid him be 'al hool' again. His only hope is to take a long winter journey to Orleans where a magician is bribed to do the work of celestial 'jogelrye'; the lover acknowledges his help:

> I, woful wrecche Aurelius,
> Thanke yow, lord, and lady myn Venus
> That me han holpen from my cares colde.

For all his expense, Dorigen prefers to destroy herself rather than see him again, and in the end, having achieved nothing, he has the magnanimity to renounce his claim.

Equally interesting is the placing of another definition of the true qualities of marriage at the opening of the Tale in which they are to be worthily represented. These lines of definition are couched in the idiom of courtly love, since here Chaucer provides an example in which Adultery is not the end of the affair. True love and marriage are not incompatible when love's servant Arveragus courts Dorigen:

> Thus hath she take hir servant and hir lord,
> Servant in love and lord in mariage,
> Than was he bothe in lordshipe and servage.

She had accepted him as her servant and as her husband where feudal love would have left her without choice. From similar basic situations the two tales reach fundamentally different conclusions about marriage. There are faults and inconsistencies to be exposed, but there is no doubt that the Franklin's perception of the need for mutual trust and respect that should go with happiness is a necessary move away from the Merchant's carnal assessment of married life's possibilities.

To read this Tale after the Merchant's is to explore the standards of human behaviour in all its facets and not to be confined to those of marriage alone. The theme of *The Franklin's Tale* resembles that of the Wife of Bath's: 'gentillesse', which emerges from Chaucer's pen (and Dante's prompting of it) as a god-given quality:

> Thy gentillesse cometh fro God allone.

And, finally, considering the purpose of the Franklin, one can at last reject the cynicism of *The Merchant's Tale* as the prejudice of a disillusioned narrator and not the faith of the controlling poet. Since the group of tales that forms a debate on marriage comes to a halt with the Franklin's contribution, it is of the highest significance that the last of the sequence should dispel the cynicism of the Merchant.

CONCLUSION

The Merchant finishes his Tale, turns to his auditors and prays them all to be glad. Why they should be so is beyond conjecture after such a sordid story. They—and we—would have been glad to have a text on which to base a more satisfactory discussion of matrimony and the moral life. Yet we can be pleased with the great subtlety of the Tale. Stating the main themes in extended analysis gives no impression of the conduct of the poem. It remains a matter for admiration that Chaucer had so wide a view of his poetic purpose as to use allegorical characters alongside real ones, to blend paganism and Christianity until one becomes a type of the other and reinforces the overall meaning.

Although the poem is rich and ambiguous, it is not at all confused. A persistent duality in it may seem to leave the meaning open to doubt, but this is not the case. Januarie calls in two counsellors, appears to have two religions, and for his philosophy seems to believe in the principle of eating his cake and still having it. He is sure that religion, which ought to be a normative influence, is sanctioning all his old predispositions and allowing him to remain at heart a whoremaster while ostensibly he is a truly married man. This is *his* confusion, and not the poet's casual permissiveness towards the reader or a general freedom of interpretation of the fable.

A pictorial image, common in medieval calendars, will make the point swiftly, although Chaucer does not himself invoke the image. The month of January is always shown as the time of carousing at the winter feast and often as a man at a table with two or even three faces looking all about him (a reference to Janus, god of doorways, who looks both ways, at the old year and the new). There is also a necessary doubleness about the zodiac sign of Gemini, the twins, under which the catastrophe in the garden is said to take place. Such images of doubleness prepare us for the poem's ending, in which what is genuinely seen is explained as being in conflict with what really happens. May assures Januarie that there was no illicit act to be spotted in the tree: it was only 'glimsing' on his part and not true vision. Because the reality is too destructive he is prepared to accept the deception, though everybody else is prepared to destroy him. It is only the surface of the poem that yields this ambiguity: everything is clearly and urgently ethical in intent.

The final work of our literature to which I would compare *The Merchant's Tale* is *Othello*. This too is made up of a web of ironies in which the central character is caught. It may be recalled that Iago, who is the supreme example of duplicity, swears by Janus before he destroys his master. In Chaucer's work there is no Iago except fortune itself, and a more guilty but equally characterless Cassio in Damyan. The style of literature to which *The Merchant's Tale* should not be compared is the category of medieval comic *fabliau*. This is a type of entertainment suitable for simple people and it is to this category that Chaucer's work has often been relegated. It may be true of any other version of the seduction in the pear tree in European literature but it is not true of this one.

In fact, this is one of Chaucer's masterpieces. If the language is at times fixed and hardened by literary convention, at others it is free and even impressionistic in its images and its sound-effects. The verse-movement is succinct and clear, performing its task with assurance. Landscape, character-portrayal and dramatic outcries are all part of the texture: its irony makes all the laughter uneasy and slightly strained. It looks so perfectly inevitable in its expression, one thinks one might almost have been born knowing it all. This is a sign that it transcends its literary analogues.

NOTE

As a companion volume to this series of Chaucer's tales the Cambridge University Press publishes *Introduction to Chaucer* in which many of the themes of this introduction will be taken further. Specific references to this volume appear in the Notes and Glossary at the back of the present Tale.

NOTE ON THE TEXT

The text which follows is based upon that of F. N. Robinson (*The Complete Works of Geoffrey Chaucer*, 2nd ed., 1957). The punctuation has been revised, with special reference to the exclamation marks. Spelling has been partly rationalized, by substituting *i* for *y* wherever the change aids the modern reader and does not affect the semantic value of the word. Thus *smylyng* becomes 'smiling', and *nyghtyngale* 'nightingale', but *wyn* (wine), *lyk* (like), and *fyr* (fire) are allowed to stand.

No accentuation has been provided in this text, for two reasons. First, because it produces a page displeasing to the eye; secondly, because it no longer seems necessary or entirely reliable in the light of modern scholarship. It is not now thought that the later works of Chaucer were written in a ten-syllable line from which no variation was permissible. The correct reading of a line of Chaucer is now seen to be more closely related to the correct reading of a comparable line of prose with phrasing suited to the rhythms of speech. This allows the reader to be more flexible in his interpretation of the line, and makes it unreasonably pedantic to provide a rigid system of accentuation.

NOTE ON PRONUNCIATION

These equivalences are intended to offer only a rough guide. For further detail, see *An Introduction to Chaucer*.

SHORT VOWELS

ă represents the sound now written *u*, as in 'cut'
ĕ as in modern 'set'
ĭ as in modern 'is'
ŏ as in modern 'top'
ŭ as in modern 'put' (not as in 'cut')
final -*e* represents the neutral vowel sound in '*a*bout' or 'atten*tio*n'. It is silent when the next word in the line begins with a vowel or an *h*.

LONG VOWELS

ā as in modern 'car' (not as in 'name')

ē (open—i.e. where the equivalent modern word is spelt with *ea*) as in modern 'there'

ē (close—i.e. where the equivalent modern word is spelt with *ee* or *e*) represents the sound now written *a* as in 'take'

ī as in modern 'machine' (not as in 'like')

ō (open—i.e. where the equivalent modern vowel is pronounced as in 'br*o*ther', 'm*oo*d', or 'g*oo*d') represents the sound now written *aw* as in 'fawn'

ō (close—i.e. where the equivalent modern vowel is pronounced as in 'road') as in modern 'note'

ŭ as in French *tu* or German *Tür*

DIPHTHONGS

ai and *ei* both roughly represent the sound now written *i* or *y* as in 'die' or 'dye'

au and *aw* both represent the sound now written *ow* or *ou* as in 'now' or 'pounce'

ou and *ow* have two pronunciations: as in *through* where the equivalent modern vowel is pronounced as in 'through' or 'mouse'; and as in *pounce* where the equivalent modern vowel is pronounced as in 'know' or 'thought'

WRITING OF VOWELS AND DIPHTHONGS

A long vowel is often indicated by doubling, as in *roote* or *eek*. The *ŭ* sound is sometimes represented by an *o* as in *yong*. The *au* sound is sometimes represented by an *a*, especially before *m* or *n*, as in *cha(u)mbre* or *cha(u)nce*.

CONSONANTS

Largely as in modern English, except that many consonants now silent were still pronounced. *Gh* was pronounced as in Scottish 'lo*ch*', and both consonants should be pronounced in such groups as the following: '*gn*acchen', '*kn*ave', 'wor*d*', 'fol*k*', '*w*rong'.

'Weping and wailing, care and oother sorwe
I knowe ynogh, on even and a-morwe,'
Quod the Marchant, 'and so doon other mo
That wedded been. I trowe that it be so,
For wel I woot it fareth so with me.
I have a wyf, the worste that may be;
For thogh the feend to hire ycoupled were,
She wolde him overmacche, I dar wel swere.
What sholde I yow reherce in special
Hir hye malice? She is a shrewe at al.   10
Ther is a long and large difference
Bitwix Grisildis grete pacience
And of my wyf the passing crueltee.
Were I unbounden, also moot I thee,
I wolde nevere eft comen in the snare.
We wedded men liven in sorwe and care.
Assaye whoso wole, and he shal finde
That I seye sooth, by Seint Thomas of Inde,
As for the moore part, I sey nat alle.
God shilde that it sholde so bifalle!   20

A, goode sire Hoost, I have ywedded bee
Thise monthes two, and moore nat, pardee;
And yet, I trowe, he that al his live
Wyflees hath been, though that men wolde him
        rive
Unto the herte, ne koude in no manere
Tellen so muchel sorwe as I now heere
Koude tellen of my wyves cursednesse!'
    'Now,' quod oure Hoost, 'Marchaunt, so God
        yow blesse,

37

Sin ye so muchel knowen of that art
30   Ful hertely I pray yow telle us part.'
     'Gladly,' quod he, 'but of myn owene soore,
For soory herte, I telle may namoore.'

THE MERCHANT'S TALE

Whilom ther was dwellinge in Lumbardye
A worthy knight, that born was of Pavie,
In which he lived in greet prosperitee;
And sixty yeer a wyflees man was hee,
And folwed ay his bodily delit
On wommen, ther as was his appetit,
As doon thise fooles that been seculeer.
And whan that he was passed sixty yeer,   40
Were it for hoolinesse or for dotage,
I kan nat seye, but swich a greet corage
Hadde this knight to been a wedded man
That day and night he dooth al that he kan
T'espien where he mighte wedded be,
Preyinge oure Lord to graunten him that he
Mighte ones knowe of thilke blisful lyf
That is bitwixe an housbonde and his wyf,
And for to live under that hooly boond
With which that first God man and womman bond. 50
'Noon oother lyf,' seyde he, 'is worth a bene;
For wedlok is so esy and so clene,
That in this world it is a paradis.'
Thus seyde this olde knight, that was so wis.
    And certeinly, as sooth as God is king,
To take a wif it is a glorious thing,
And namely whan a man is oold and hoor;
Thanne is a wyf the fruit of his tresor.
Thanne sholde he take a yong wif and a feir,
On which he mighte engendren him an heir,   60
And lede his lyf in joye and in solas,

Where as thise bacheleris singe 'allas,'
Whan that they finden any adversitee
In love, which nis but childissh vanitee.
And trewely it sit wel to be so,
That bacheleris have often peyne and wo;
On brotel ground they builde, and brotelnesse
They finde, whan they wene sikernesse.
They live but as a brid or as a beest,
70   In libertee, and under noon arreest;
Ther as a wedded man in his estaat
Liveth a lyf blisful and ordinaat,
Under this yok of mariage ybounde.
Wel may his herte in joy and blisse habounde,
For who kan be so buxom as a wyf?
Who is so trewe, and eek so ententif
To kepe him, sik and hool, as is his make?
For wele or wo she wole him nat forsake;
She nis nat wery him to love and serve,
80   Thogh that he lye bedrede, til he sterve.
And yet somme clerkes seyn it nis nat so,
Of whiche he Theofraste is oon of tho.
What force though Theofraste liste lye?
'Ne take no wyf,' quod he, 'for housbondrye,
As for to spare in houshold thy dispence.
A trewe servant dooth moore diligence
Thy good to kepe, than thyn owene wyf,
For she wol claime half part al hir lyf.
And if that thou be sik, so God me save,
90   Thy verray freendes, or a trewe knave,
Wol kepe thee bet than she that waiteth ay
After thy good and hath doon many a day.
And if thou take a wyf unto thyn hoold,

Ful lightly maystow been a cokewold.'
This sentence, and an hundred thinges worse,
Writeth this man, ther God his bones corse!
But take no kep of al swich vanitee;
Deffie Theofraste, and herke me.

   A wyf is Goddes yifte verraily;
Alle othere manere yiftes hardily,   100
As londes, rentes, pasture, or commune,
Or moebles, alle been yiftes of Fortune,
That passen as a shadwe upon a wal.
But drede nat, if pleynly speke I shal,
A wif wol laste, and in thyn hous endure,
Wel lenger than thee list, paraventure.

   Mariage is a ful greet sacrement.
He which that hath no wyf, I holde him shent;
He liveth helplees and al desolat,—
I speke of folk in seculer estaat.   110
And herke why, I sey nat this for noght,
That womman is for mannes helpe ywroght.
The hie God, whan he hadde Adam maked,
And saugh him al allone, bely-naked;
God of his grete goodnesse seyde than,
'Lat us now make an helpe unto this man
Lyk to himself'; and thanne He made him Eve.
Heere may ye se, and heerby may ye preve,
That wyf is mannes helpe and his confort;
His paradis terrestre, and his disport.   120
So buxom and so vertuous is she,
They moste nedes live in unitee.
O flessh they been, and o fleesh, as I gesse,
Hath but oon herte, in wele and in distresse.

   A wyf, a, Seinte Marie, *benedicite,*

How mighte a man han any adversitee
That hath a wyf? Certes, I kan nat seye.
The blisse which that is bitwixe hem tweye
Ther may no tonge telle, or herte thinke.
If he be povre, she helpeth him to swinke;
She kepeth his good, and wasteth never a deel;
Al that hire housbonde lust, hire liketh weel;
She seith nat ones 'nay', whan he seith 'ye.'
'Do this,' seith he; 'Al redy, sire,' seith she.
O blisful ordre of wedlok precious,
Thou art so murye, and eek so vertuous,
And so commended and appreved eek
That every man that halt him worth a leek,
Upon his bare knees oughte al his lyf
Thanken his God that him hath sent a wyf,
Or elles preye to God him for to sende
A wyf, to laste unto his lives ende.
For thanne his lyf is set in sikernesse;
He may nat be deceyved, as I gesse,
So that he werke after his wyves reed.
Thanne may he boldely beren up his heed,
They been so trewe, and therwithal so wise;
For which, if thou wolt werken as the wise,
Do alwey so as wommen wol thee rede.

Lo, how that Jacob, as thise clerkes rede,
By good conseil of his mooder Rebekke,
Boond the kides skin aboute his nekke,
For which his fadres benison he wan.

Lo Judith, as the storic eek telle kan,
By wis conseil she Goddes peple kepte,
And slow him Olofernus, whil he slepte.

Lo Abigail, by good conseil, how she

Saved hir housbonde Nabal, whan that he
Sholde han be slain; and looke, Ester also
By good conseil delivered out of wo   160
The peple of God, and made him Mardochee
Of Assuere enhaunced for to be.

Ther nis no thing in gree superlatif,
As seith Senek, above an humble wyf.

Suffre thy wives tonge, as Catoun bit;
She shal comande, and thou shalt suffren it,
And yet she wole obeye of curteisye.
A wif is kepere of thyn housbondrye;
Wel may the sike man biwaille and wepe,
Ther as ther nis no wyf the hous to kepe.   170
I warne thee, if wisely thou wolt wirche,
Love wel thy wyf, as Crist loved his chirche.
If thou lovest thyself, thou lovest thy wyf;
No man hateth his flessh, but in his lyf
He fostreth it, and therfore bidde I thee,
Cherisse thy wyf, or thou shalt nevere thee.
Housbonde and wyf, what so men jape or pleye,
Of worldly folk holden the siker weye;
They been so knit ther may noon harm bitide,
And namely upon the wyves side.   180
For which this Januarie, of whom I tolde,
Considered hath, inwith his dayes olde,
The lusty lyf, the vertuous quiete,
That is in mariage hony-sweete;
And for his freendes on a day he sente,
To tellen hem th'effect of his entente.

With face sad his tale he hath hem toold.
He seyde, 'Freendes, I am hoor and oold,
And almoost, God woot, on my pittes brinke;

43

190   Upon my soule somwhat moste I thinke.
I have my body folily despended;
Blessed be God that it shal been amended.
For I wol be, certeyn, a wedded man,
And that anoon in al the haste I kan.
Unto som mayde fair and tendre of age,
I prey yow, shapeth for my mariage
Al sodeynly, for I wol nat abide;
And I wol fonde t'espien, on my side,
To whom I may be wedded hastily.

200   But forasmuche as ye been mo than I,
Ye shullen rather swich a thing espyen
Than I, and where me best were to allyen.

    But o thing warne I yow, my freendes deere,
I wol noon oold wyf han in no manere.
She shal nat passe twenty yeer, certain;
Oold fissh and yong flessh wolde I have ful fain.
Bet is,' quod he, 'a pyk than a pikerel,
And bet than old boef is the tendre veel.
I wol no womman thritty yeer of age;

210   It is but bene-straw and greet forage.
And eek thise olde widwes, God it woot,
They konne so muchel craft on Wades boot,
So muchel broken harm, whan that hem leste,
That with hem sholde I nevere live in reste.
For sondry scoles maken sotile clerkis;
Womman of manye scoles half a clerk is.
But certeynly, a yong thing may men gye,
Right as men may warm wex with handes plye.
Wherfore I sey yow pleynly, in a clause,

220   I wol noon oold wyf han right for this cause.
For if so were I hadde swich mischaunce,

That I in hire ne koude han no plesaunce,
Thanne sholde I lede my lyf in avoutrye,
And go streight to the devel, whan I die.
Ne children sholde I none upon hire geten;
Yet were me levere houndes had me eten,
Than that myn heritage sholde falle
In straunge hand, and this I telle yow alle.
I dote nat, I woot the cause why
Men sholde wedde, and forthermoore woot I,   230
Ther speketh many a man of mariage
That woot namoore of it than woot my page,
For whiche causes man sholde take a wyf.
If he ne may nat liven chaast his lyf,
Take him a wyf with greet devocioun,
By cause of leveful procreacioun
Of children, to th'onour of God above,
And nat oonly for paramour or love;
And for they sholde leccherye eschue,
And yelde hir dette whan that it is due;   240
Or for that ech of hem sholde helpen oother
In meschief, as a suster shal the brother;
And live in chastitee ful holily.
But sires, by youre leve, that am nat I.
For, God be thanked, I dar make avaunt,
I feele my lymes stark and suffisaunt
To do al that a man bilongeth to;
I woot myselven best what I may do.
Though I be hoor, I fare as dooth a tree
That blosmeth er that fruit ywoxen bee;   250
And blosmy tree nis neither drye ne deed.
I feele me nowhere hoor but on myn heed;
Myn herte and alle my lymes been as grene

As laurer thurgh the yeer is for to sene.
And sin that ye han herd al myn entente,
I prey yow to my wil ye wole assente.'
    Diverse men diversely him tolde
Of mariage manye ensamples olde.
Somme blamed it, somme preysed it, certeyn;
But atte laste, shortly for to seyn,
As al day falleth altercacioun
Bitwixen freendes in disputisoun,
Ther fil a strif bitwixe his bretheren two,
Of whiche that oon was cleped Placebo,
Justinus soothly called was that oother.
    Placebo seyde, 'O Januarie, brother,
Ful litel nede hadde ye, my lord so deere,
Conseil to axe of any that is heere,
But that ye been so ful of sapience
That yow ne liketh, for youre heighe prudence,
To weyven fro the word of Salomon.
This word seyde he unto us everychon:
"Wirk alle thing by conseil," thus seyde he,
"And thanne shaltow nat repente thee."
But though that Salomon spak swich a word,
Myn owene deere brother and my lord,
So wisly God my soule bringe at reste,
I holde youre owene conseil is the beste.
For, brother myn, of me taak this motif,
I have now been a court-man al my lyf,
And God it woot, though I unworthy be,
I have stonden in ful greet degree
Abouten lordes of ful heigh estaat;
Yet hadde I nevere with noon of hem debaat.
I nevere hem contraried, trewely;

I woot wel that my lord kan moore than I.
With that he seith, I holde it ferme and stable;
I seye the same, or elles thing semblable.
A ful greet fool is any conseillour
That serveth any lord of heigh honour,   290
That dar presume, or elles thenken it,
That his conseil sholde passe his lordes wit.
Nay, lordes been no fooles, by my fay.
Ye han youreselven shewed heer to-day
So heigh sentence, so holily and weel,
That I consente and conferme everydeel
Youre wordes alle and youre opinioun.
By God, ther nis no man in al this toun,
Ne in Itaille, that koude bet han said!
Crist halt him of this conseil ful wel apaid.   300
And trewely, it is an heigh corage
Of any man that stapen is in age
To take a yong wif; by my fader kin,
Youre herte hangeth on a joly pin!
Dooth now in this matiere right as yow leste,
For finally I holde it for the beste.'

   Justinus, that ay stille sat and herde,
Right in this wise he to Placebo answerde:
'Now, brother myn, be pacient, I preye,
Sin ye han seyd, and herkneth what I seye.   310
Senek, amonges othere wordes wise,
Seith that a man oghte him right wel avise
To whom he yeveth his lond or his catel.
And sin I oghte avise me right wel
To whom I yeve my good awey fro me,
Wel muchel moore I oghte avised be
To whom I yeve my body for alwey.

47

I warne yow wel, it is no childes pley
To take a wyf withouten avisement.
320   Men moste enquere, this is myn assent,
Wher she be wys, or sobre, or dronkelewe,
Or proud, or elles ootherweys a shrewe,
A chidestere, or wastour of thy good,
Or riche, or poore, or elles mannissh wood.
Al be it so that no man finden shal
Noon in this world that trotteth hool in al,
Ne man, ne beest, swich as men koude devise;
But nathelees it oghte ynough suffise
With any wyf, if so were that she hadde
330   Mo goode thewes than hire vices badde;
And al this axeth leyser for t'enquere.
For, God it woot, I have wept many a teere
Ful prively, sin I have had a wyf.
Preyse whoso wole a wedded mannes lyf,
Certein I finde in it but cost and care
And observances, of alle blisses bare.
And yet, God woot, my neighebores aboute,
And namely of wommen many a route,
Seyn that I have the mooste stedefast wyf,
340   And eek the mekeste oon that bereth lyf;
But I woot best where wringeth me my sho.
Ye mowe, for me, right as yow liketh do;
Aviseth yow—ye been a man of age—
How that ye entren into mariage,
And namely with a yong wyf and a fair.
By him that made water, erthc, and air,
The yongeste man that is in al this route
Is bisy ynough to bringen it aboute
To han his wyf allone. Trusteth me,

Ye shul nat plescn hire fully yeres thre,—   350
This is to seyn, to doon hire ful plesaunce.
A wif axeth ful many an observaunce.
I prey yow that ye be nat yvele apaid.'
   'Wel,' quod this Januarie, 'and hastow said?
Straw for thy Senek, and for thy proverbes!
I counte nat a panyer ful of herbes
Of scole-termes. Wiser men than thow,
As thou hast herd, assenteden right now
To my purpos. Placebo, what sey ye?'
   'I seye it is a cursed man,' quod he,   360
'That letteth matrimoigne, sikerly.'
And with that word they risen sodeynly,
And been assented fully that he sholde
Be wedded whanne him liste, and where he wolde.
   Heigh fantasye and curious bisynesse
Fro day to day gan in the soule impresse
Of Januarie aboute his mariage.
Many fair shap and many a fair visage
Ther passeth thurgh his herte night by night,
As whoso tooke a mirour, polisshed bright,   370
And sette it in a commune market-place,
Thanne sholde he se ful many a figure pace
By his mirour: and in the same wise
Gan Januarie inwith his thoght devise
Of maidens whiche that dwelten him biside.
He wiste nat wher that he mighte abide.
For if that oon have beaute in hir face,
Another stant so in the peples grace
For hire sadnesse and hire beningnitee
That of the peple grettest voys hath she;   380
And somme were riche, and hadden badde name.

But nathelees, bitwixe ernest and game,
He atte laste apointed him on oon,
And leet alle othere from his herte goon,
And chees hire of his owene auctoritee;
For love is blind alday, and may nat see.
And whan that he was in his bed ybroght,
He purtreyed in his herte and in his thoght
Hir fresshe beautee and hir age tendre,
Hir middel smal, hire armes longe and sklendre,
Hir wise governaunce, hir gentillesse,
Hir wommanly beringe, and hire sadnesse.
And whan that he on hire was condescended,
Him thoughte his choys mighte nat ben amended.
For whan that he himself concluded hadde,
Him thoughte ech oother mannes wit so badde
That inpossible it were to repplye
Again his choys, this was his fantasye.
His freendes sente he to, at his instaunce,
And preyed hem to doon him that plesaunce,
That hastily they wolden to him come;
He wolde abregge hir labour, alle and some.
Nedeth namoore for hem to go ne ride;
He was apointed ther he wolde abide.

Placebo cam, and eek his freendes soone,
And alderfirst he bad hem alle a boone,
That noon of hem none argumentes make
Again the purpos which that he hath take,
Which purpos was plesant to God, seyde he,
And verray ground of his prosperitee.

He seyde ther was a maiden in the toun,
Which that of beautee hadde greet renoun,
Al were it so she were of smal degree;

Suffiseth him hir yowthe and hir beautee.
Which maide, he seyde, he wolde han to his wyf,
To lede in ese and hoolinesse his lyf;
And thanked God that he mighte han hire al,
That no wight his blisse parten shal.
And preyed hem to laboure in this nede,
And shapen that he faille nat to spede;   420
For thanne, he seyde, his spirit was at ese.
'Thanne is,' quod he, 'no thing may me displese,
Save o thing priketh in my conscience,
The which I wol reherce in youre presence.

   I have,' quod he, 'herd seyd, ful yoore ago,
Ther may no man han parfite blisses two—
This is to seye, in erthe and eek in hevene.
For though he kepe him fro the sinnes sevene,
And eek from every branche of thilke tree,
Yet is ther so parfit felicitee   430
And so greet ese and lust in mariage,
That evere I am agast now in myn age
That I shal lede now so myrie a lyf,
So delicat, withouten wo and stryf,
That I shal have myn hevene in erthe heere.
For sith that verray hevene is boght so deere
With tribulacion and greet penaunce,
How sholde I thanne, that live in swich plesaunce
As alle wedded men doon with hire wyvys,
Come to the blisse ther Crist eterne on live is?   440
This is my drede, and ye, my bretheren tweye,
Assoilleth me this question, I preye.'

   Justinus, which that hated his folye,
Answerde anon right in his japerye;
And for he wolde his longe tale abregge,

He wolde noon auctoritee allegge,
But seyde, 'Sire, so ther be noon obstacle
Oother than this, God of his high miracle
And of his mercy may so for yow wirche
That, er ye have youre right of hooly chirche,
Ye may repente of wedded mannes lyf,
In which ye seyn ther is no wo ne stryf.
And elles, God forbede but he sente
A wedded man him grace to repente
Wel ofte rather than a sengle man.
And therfore, sire—the beste reed I kan—
Dispeire yow noght, but have in youre memorie,
Paraunter she may be youre purgatorie.
She may be Goddes meene and Goddes whippe;
Thanne shal youre soule up to hevene skippe
Swifter than dooth an arwe out of a bowe.
I hope to God, herafter shul ye knowe
That ther nis no so greet felicitee
In mariage, ne nevere mo shal bee,
That yow shal lette of youre savacion,
So that ye use, as skile is and reson,
The lustes of youre wyf attemprely,
And that ye plese hire nat to amorously,
And that ye kepe yow eek from oother sinne.
My tale is doon, for my wit is thinne.
Beth nat agast herof, my brother deere,
But lat us waden out of this mateere.
The Wyf of Bathe, if ye han understonde,
Of mariage, which we have on honde,
Declared hath ful wel in litel space.
Fareth now wel, God have yow in his grace.'
    And with this word this Justin and his brother

450

460

470

Han take hir leve, and ech of hem of oother.
For whan they saughe that it moste nedes be,
They wroghten so, by sly and wys tretee, 480
That she, this maiden, which that Mayus highte,
As hastily as evere that she mighte,
Shal wedded be unto this Januarie.
I trowe it were to longe yow to tarie,
If I yow tolde of every scrit and bond
By which that she was feffed in his lond,
Or for to herknen of hir riche array.
But finally ycomen is the day
That to the chirche bothe be they went
For to receyve the hooly sacrement. 490
Forth comth the preest, with stole aboute his nekke,
And bad hire be lyk Sarra and Rebekke
In wisdom and in trouthe of mariage;
And seyde his orisons, as is usage,
And croucheth hem, and bad God sholde hem blesse,
And made al siker ynogh with hoolinesse.

    Thus been they wedded with solempnitee,
And at the feeste sitteth he and she
With othere worthy folk upon the deys.
Al ful of joye and blisse is the paleys, 500
And ful of instrumentz and of vitaille,
The mooste deyntevous of al Itaille:
Biforn hem stoode instrumentz of swich soun
That Orpheus, ne of Thebes Amphioun,
Ne maden nevere swich a melodye.
At every cours thanne cam loud minstralcye,
That nevere tromped Joab for to heere,
Nor he Theodomas, yet half so cleere,
At Thebes, whan the citee was in doute.

53

510 Bacus the wyn hem shinketh al aboute,
And Venus laugheth upon every wight,
For Januarie was bicome hir knight,
And wolde bothe assayen his corage
In libertee, and eek in mariage;
And with hire fyrbrond in hire hand aboute
Daunceth biforn the bride and al the route.
And certeinly, I dar right wel seyn this,
Ymeneus, that god of wedding is,
Saugh nevere his lyf so myrie a wedded man.

520 Hoold thou thy pees, thou poete Marcian,
That writest us that ilke wedding murie
Of hire Philologie and him Mercurie,
And of the songes that the Muses songe.
To smal is bothe thy penne, and eek thy tonge,
For to descriven of this mariage:
Whan tendre youthe hath wedded stouping age,
Ther is swich mirthe that it may nat be writen.
Assayeth it youreself, thanne may ye witen
If that I lie or noon in this matiere.

530   Mayus, that sit with so beningne a chiere,
Hire to biholde it semed faierye.
Queene Ester looked nevere with swich an ye
On Assuer, so meke a look hath she.
I may yow nat devise al hir beautee.
But thus muche of hire beautee telle I may,
That she was lyk the brighte morwe of May,
Fulfild of alle beautee and plesaunce.
    This Januarie is ravisshed in a traunce
At every time he looked on hir face;

540 But in his herte he gan hire to manace
That he that night in armes wolde hire streyne

Harder than evere Paris dide Eleyne.
But nathelees yet hadde he greet pitee
That thilke night offenden hire moste he,
And thoughte, 'Allas, O tendre creature,
Now wolde God ye mighte wel endure
Al my corage, it is so sharp and keene.
I am agast ye shul it nat susteene.
But God forbede that I dide al my might!
Now wolde God that it were woxen night,   550
And that the night wolde lasten everemo.
I wolde that al this peple were ago.'
And finally he dooth al his labour,
As he best mighte, savinge his honour,
To haste hem fro the mete in subtil wise.

    The time cam that resoun was to rise;
And after that men daunce and drinken faste,
And spices al aboute the hous they caste;
And ful of joye and blisse is every man,—
Al but a squier, highte Damyan,   560
Which carf biforn the knight ful many a day.
He was so ravisshed on his lady May
That for the verray peyne he was ny wood.
Almoost he swelte and swowned ther he stood,
So soore hath Venus hurt him with hire brond,
As that she bar it daunsinge in hire hond;
And to his bed he wente him hastily.
Namoore of him as at this time speke I,
But there I lete him wepe ynogh and pleyne,
Til fresshe May wol rewen on his peyne.   570

    O perilous fyr, that in the bedstraw bredeth;
O famulier foo, that his service bedeth;
O servant traitour, false hoomly hewe,

55

Lyk to the naddre in bosom sly untrewe,
God shilde us alle from youre aqueyntaunce.
O Januarie, dronken in plesaunce
In mariage, se how thy Damyan,
Thyn owene squier and thy borne man,
Entendeth for to do thee vileynye.
God graunte thee thyn hoomly fo t'espye.
For in this world nis worse pestilence
Than hoomly foo al day in thy presence.

   Parfourned hath the sonne his ark diurne;
No lenger may the body of him sojurne
On th'orisonte, as in that latitude.
Night with his mantel, that is derk and rude,
Gan oversprede the hemisperie aboute;
For which departed is this lusty route
Fro Januarie, with thank on every side.
Hoom to hir houses lustily they ride,
Where as they doon hir thinges as hem leste,
And whan they sye hir time, goon to reste.
Soone after that, this hastif Januarie
Wolde go to bedde, he wolde no lenger tarye.
He drinketh ypocras, clarree, and vernage
Of spices hoote, t'encreessen his corage;
And many a letuarie hath he ful fyn,
Swiche as the cursed monk, daun Constantin,
Hath writen in his book *De Coitu*;
To eten hem alle he nas no thing eschu.
And to his privee freendes thus seyde he:
'For Goddes love, as soone as it may be,
Lat voiden al this hous in curteys wise.'
And they han doon right as he wol devise.
Men drinken, and the travers drawe anon.

580

590

600

56

The bride was broght abedde as stille as stoon;
And whan the bed was with the preest yblessed,
Out of the chambre hath every wight him dressed;
And Januarie hath faste in armes take
His fresshe May, his paradis, his make.   610
He lulleth hire, he kisseth hire ful ofte;
With thikke brustles of his berd unsofte,
Lyk to the skin of houndfissh, sharp as brere—
For he was shave al newe in his manere—
He rubbeth hire aboute hir tendre face,
And seyde thus, 'Allas, I moot trespace
To yow, my spouse, and yow greetly offende,
Er time come that I wil doun descende.
But nathelees, considereth this,' quod he,
'Ther nis no werkman, whatsoevere he be,   620
That may bothe werke wel and hastily;
This wol be doon at leyser parfitly.
It is no fors how longe that we pleye;
In trewe wedlok coupled be we tweye;
And blessed be the yok that we been inne,
For in oure actes we mowe do no sinne.
A man may do no sinne with his wyf,
Ne hurte himselven with his owene knyf;
For we han leve to pleye us by the lawe.'
Thus laboureth he til that the day gan dawe;   630
And thanne he taketh a sop in fyn clarree,
And upright in his bed thanne sitteth he,
And after that he sang ful loude and cleere,
And kiste his wif, and made wantown cheere.
He was al coltissh, ful of ragerye,
And ful of jargon as a flekked pye.
The slakke skin aboute his nekke shaketh.

57

Whil that he sang, so chaunteth he and craketh.
But God woot what that May thoughte in hir herte,

640 Whan she him saugh up sittinge in his sherte,
In his night-cappe, and with his nekke lene;
She preyseth nat his pleying worth a bene.
Thanne seide he thus, 'My reste wol I take;
Now day is come, I may no lenger wake.'
And doun he leyde his heed, and sleep til prime.
And afterward, whan that he saugh his time,
Up riseth Januarie; but fresshe May
Heeld hire chambre unto the fourthe day,
As usage is of wives for the beste.

650 For every labour somtime moot han reste,
Or elles longe may he nat endure;
This is to seyn, no lives creature,
Be it of fissh, or brid, or beest, or man.

Now wol I speke of woful Damyan,
That langwissheth for love, as ye shul heere;
Therfore I speke to him in this manere:
I seye, 'O sely Damyan, allas,
Andswere to my demaunde, as in this cas.
How shaltow to thy lady, fresshe May,

660 Telle thy wo? She wole alwey seye nay.
Eek if thou speke, she wol thy wo biwreye.
God be thyn helpe, I kan no bettre seye.'

This sike Damyan in Venus fyr
So brenneth that he dieth for desir,
For which he putte his lyf in aventure.
No lenger mighte he in this wise endure,
But prively a penner gan he borwe,
And in a lettre wroot he al his sorwe,
In manere of a compleynt or a lay,

Unto his faire, fresshe lady May;　　　　　　670
And in a purs of silk, heng on his sherte
He hath it put, and leyde it at his herte.

　　The moone, that at noon was thilke day
That Januarie hath wedded fresshe May
In two of Tawr, was into Cancre gliden;
So longe hath Mayus in hir chambre abiden,
As custume is unto thise nobles alle.
A bride shal nat eten in the halle
Til dayes foure, or thre dayes atte leeste,
Ypassed been; thanne lat hire go to feeste.　　680
The fourthe day compleet fro noon to noon,
Whan that the heighe masse was ydoon,
In halle sit this Januarie and May,
As fressh as is the brighte someres day.
And so bifel how that this goode man
Remembred him upon this Damyan,
And seyde, 'Seynte Marie, how may this be,
That Damyan entendeth nat to me?
Is he ay sik, or how may this bitide?'
His squieres, whiche that stooden ther biside,　　690
Excused him by cause of his siknesse,
Which letted him to doon his bisynesse;
Noon oother cause mighte make him tarye.

　　'That me forthinketh,' quod this Januarie,
'He is a gentil squier, by my trouthe;
If that he deyde, it were harm and routhe.
He is as wys, discreet, and as secree
As any man I woot of his degree,
And therto manly, and eek servisable,
And for to been a thrifty man right able.　　700
But after mete, as soone as evere I may,

I wol myself visite him, and eek May,
To doon him al the confort that I kan.'
And for that word him blessed every man,
That of his bountee and his gentillesse
He wolde so conforten in siknesse
His squier, for it was a gentil dede.
'Dame,' quod this Januarie, 'taak good hede,
At after-mete ye with youre wommen alle,
Whan ye han been in chambre out of this halle,
That alle ye go se this Damyan.
Dooth him disport—he is a gentil man;
And telleth him that I wol him visite,
Have I no thing but rested me a lite;
And spede yow faste, for I wole abide
Til that ye slepe faste by my side.'
And with that word he gan to him to calle
A squier, that was marchal of his halle,
And tolde him certeyn thinges, what he wolde.

This fresshe May hath streight hir wey yholde,
With alle hir wommen, unto Damyan.
Doun by his beddes side sit she than,
Confortinge him as goodly as she may.
This Damyan, whan that his time he say,
In secree wise his purs and eek his bille,
In which that he ywriten hadde his wille,
Hath put into hire hand, withouten moore,
Save that he siketh wonder depe and soore,
And softely to hire right thus seyde he:
'Mercy, and that ye nat discovere me,
For I am deed if that this thing be kid.'
This purs hath she inwith hir bosom hid,
And wente hire wey; ye gete namoore of me.

But unto Januarie ycomen is she,
That on his beddes side sit ful softe.
He taketh hire, and kisseth hire ful ofte,
And leyde him doun to slepe, and that anon.
She feyned hire as that she moste gon
Ther as ye woot that every wight moot neede;
And whan she of this bille hath taken heede,   740
She rente it al to cloutes atte laste,
And in the privee softely it caste.

   Who studieth now but faire fresshe May?
Adoun by olde Januarie she lay,
That sleep til that the coughe hath him awaked.
Anon he preyde hire strepen hire al naked;
He wolde of hire, he seyde, han som plesaunce,
And seyde hir clothes dide him encombraunce,
And she obeyeth, be hire lief or looth.
But lest that precious folk be with me wrooth,   750
How that he wroghte, I dar nat to yow telle;
Or wheither hire thoughte it paradis or helle,
But heere I lete hem werken in hir wise
Til evensong rong, and that they moste arise.

   Were it by destinee or aventure,
Were it by influence or by nature,
Or constellacion, that in swich estaat
The hevene stood, that time fortunaat
Was for to putte a bille of Venus werkes—
For alle thing hath time, as seyn thise clerkes—   760
To any womman, for to gete hire love,
I kan nat seye; but grete God above,
That knoweth that noon act is causelees,
He deme of al, for I wole holde my pees.
But sooth is this, how that this fresshe May

Hath take swich impression that day
Of pitee of this sike Damyan,
That from hire herte she ne drive kan
The remembrance for to doon him ese.
770 'Certeyn,' thoghte she, 'whom that this thing disple
I rekke noght, for heere I him assure
To love him best of any creature,
Though he namoore hadde than his sherte.'
Lo, pitee renneth soone in gentil herte.

Heere may ye se how excellent franchise
In wommen is, whan they hem narwe avise.
Som tyrant is, as ther be many oon,
That hath an herte as hard as any stoon,
Which wolde han lat him sterven in the place
780 Wel rather than han graunted him hire grace;
And hem rejoysen in hire crueel pride,
And rekke nat to been an homicide.

This gentil May, fulfilled of pitee,
Right of hire hand a lettre made she,
In which she graunteth him hire verray grace.
Ther lakketh noght, oonly but day and place,
Wher that she mighte unto his lust suffise;
For it shal be right as he wole devise.
And whan she saugh hir time, upon a day,
790 To visite this Damyan gooth May,
And sotilly this lettre doun she threste
Under his pilwe, rede it if him leste.
She taketh him by the hand, and harde him twiste
So secrely that no wight of it wiste,
And bad him been al hool, and forth she wente
To Januarie, whan that he for hire sente.

Up riseth Damyan the nexte morwe;

62

Al passed was his siknesse and his sorwe.
He kembeth him, he preyneth him and piketh,
He dooth al that his lady lust and liketh; 800
And eek to Januarie he gooth as lowe
As evere dide a dogge for the bowe.
He is so plesant unto every man
(For craft is al, whoso that do it kan)
That every wight is fain to speke him good;
And fully in his lady grace he stood.
Thus lete I Damyan aboute his nede,
And in my tale forth I wol procede.

Somme clerkes holden that felicitee
Stant in delit, and therfore certeyn he, 810
This noble Januarie, with al his might,
In honest wise, as longeth to a knight,
Shoop him to live ful deliciously.
His housinge, his array, as honestly
To his degree was maked as a kinges.
Amonges othere of his honeste thinges,
He made a gardyn, walled al with stoon;
So fair a gardyn woot I nowher noon.
For, out of doute, I verraily suppose
That he that wroot the Romance of the Rose 820
Ne koude of it the beautee wel devise;
Ne Priapus ne mighte nat suffise,
Though he be god of gardyns, for to telle
The beautee of the gardyn and the welle,
That stood under a laurer alwey grene.
Ful ofte time he Pluto and his queene,
Proserpina, and al hire faierye,
Disporten hem and maken melodye
Aboute that welle, and daunced, as men tolde.

830   This noble knight, this Januarie the olde,
Swich deyntee hath in it to walke and pleye,
That he wol no wight suffren bere the keye
Save he himself; for of the smale wiket
He baar alwey of silver a cliket,
With which, whan that him leste, he it unshette.
And whan he wolde paye his wyf hir dette
In somer seson, thider wolde he go,
And May his wyf, and no wight but they two;
And thinges whiche that were nat doon abedde,
840 He in the gardyn parfourned hem and spedde.
And in this wise, many a murye day,
Lived this Januarie and fresshe May.
But worldly joye may nat alwey dure
To Januarie, ne to no creature.

    O sodeyn hap, o thou Fortune unstable!
Lyk to the scorpion so deceyvable,
That flaterest with thyn heed whan thou wolt stin
Thy tail is deeth, thurgh thyn envenyminge.
O brotil joye, o sweete venym queynte!
850 O monstre, that so subtilly kanst peynte
Thy yiftes under hewe of stidefastnesse,
That thou deceyvest bothe moore and lesse.
Why hastow Januarie thus deceyved,
That haddest him for thy fulle freend receyved?
And now thou hast biraft him bothe his yen,
For sorwe of which desireth he to dien.

    Allas, this noble Januarie free,
Amidde his lust and his prosperitee,
Is woxen blind, and that al sodeynly.
860 He wepeth and he waileth pitously;
And therwithal the fyr of jalousie,

Lest that his wyf sholde falle in som folye,
So brente his herte that he wolde fain
That som man bothe hire and him had slain.
For neither after his deeth, nor in his lyf,
Ne wolde he that she were love ne wyf,
But evere live as widwe in clothes blake,
Soul as the turtle that lost hath hire make.
But atte laste, after a month or tweye,
His sorwe gan aswage, sooth to seye;   870
For whan he wiste it may noon oother be,
He paciently took his adversitee,
Save, out of doute, he may nat forgoon
That he nas jalous everemoore in oon;
Which jalousye it was so outrageous,
That neither in halle, n'in noon oother hous,
Ne in noon oother place, neverthemo,
He nolde suffre hire for to ride or go,
But if that he had hond on hire alway;
For which ful ofte wepeth fresshe May,   880
That loveth Damyan so beningnely
That she moot outher dien sodeynly,
Or elles she moot han him as hir leste.
She waiteth whan hir herte wolde breste.

Upon that oother side Damyan
Bicomen is the sorwefulleste man
That evere was; for neither night ne day
Ne mighte he speke a word to fresshe May,
As to his purpos, of no swich mateere,
But if that Januarie moste it heere,   890
That hadde an hand upon hire everemo.
But nathelees, by writing to and fro,
And privee signes, wiste he what she mente,

And she knew eek the fin of his entente.

O Januarie, what mighte it thee availle,
Thogh thou mighte se as fer as shippes saille?
For as good is blind deceyved be
As to be deceyved whan a man may se.

Lo, Argus, which that hadde an hondred yen,
900 For al that evere he koude poure or pryen,
Yet was he blent, and, God woot, so been mo,
That wenen wisly that it be nat so.
Passe over is an ese, I sey namoore.

This fresshe May, that I spak of so yoore,
In warm wex hath emprented the cliket
That Januarie bar of the smale wiket,
By which into his gardyn ofte he wente,
And Damyan, that knew al hire entente,
The cliket countrefeted prively.
910 Ther nis namoore to seye, but hastily
Som wonder by this cliket shal bitide,
Which ye shul heeren, if ye wole abide.

O noble Ovide, ful sooth seystou, God woot,
What sleighte is it, thogh it be long and hoot,
That Love nil finde it out in som manere?
By Piramus and Tesbee may men leere;
Thogh they were kept ful longe streite overal,
They been accorded, rowninge thurgh a wal,
Ther no wight koude han founde out swich a sleighte.
920 But now to purpos: er that dayes eighte
Were passed, er the month of Juin, bifil
That Januarie hath caught so greet a wil,
Thurgh egging of his wyf, him for to pleye
In his gardyn, and no wight but they tweye,
That in a morwe unto his May seith he:

'Ris up, my wyf, my love, my lady free,
The turtles vois is herd, my dowve sweete;
The winter is goon with alle his reynes weete.
Com forth now, with thine eyen columbin,
How fairer been thy brestes than is wyn.   930
The gardyn is enclosed al aboute;
Com forth, my white spouse, out of doute
Thou hast me wounded in myn herte, O wyf,
No spot of thee ne knew I al my lyf.
Com forth, and lat us taken oure disport;
I chees thee for my wyf and my confort.'
    Swiche olde lewed wordes used he.
On Damyan a signe made she,
That he sholde go biforn with his cliket.
This Damyan thanne hath opened the wiket,   940
And in he stirte, and that in swich manere
That no wight mighte it se neither yheere,
And stille he sit under a bussh anon.
    This Januarie, as blind as is a stoon,
With Mayus in his hand, and no wight mo,
Into his fresshe gardyn is ago,
And clapte to the wiket sodeynly,
    'Now wyf,' quod he, 'heere nis but thou and I,
That art the creature that I best love.
For by that Lord that sit in hevene above,   950
Levere ich hadde to dien on a knyf,
Than thee offende, trewe deere wyf!
For Goddes sake, thenk how I thee chees,
Noght for no coveitise, doutelees,
But oonly for the love I had to thee.
And though that I be oold, and may nat see,
Beth to me trewe, and I wol telle yow why.

67

Thre thinges, certes, shal ye winne therby:
First, love of Crist, and to youreself honour,
960 And al myn heritage, toun and tour;
I yeve it yow, maketh chartres as yow leste;
This shal be doon to-morwe er sonne reste,
So wisly God my soule bringe in blisse.
I prey yow first, in covenant ye me kisse;
And though that I be jalous, wite me noght.
Ye been so depe enprented in my thoght
That, whan that I considere youre beautee,
And therwithal the unlikly elde of me,
I may nat, certes, though I sholde die,
970 Forbere to been out of youre compaignye
For verray love; this is withouten doute.
Now kis me, wyf, and lat us rome aboute.'

    This fresshe May, whan she thise wordes herde,
Beningnely to Januarie answerde,
But first and forward she bigan to wepe.
'I have,' quod she, 'a soule for to kepe
As wel as ye, and also myn honour,
And of my wifhod thilke tendre flour,
Which that I have assured in youre hond,
980 Whan that the preest to yow my body bond;
Wherfore I wole answere in this manere,
By the leve of yow, my lord so deere:
I prey to God that nevere dawe the day
That I ne sterve, as foule as womman may,
If evere I do unto my kin that shame,
Or elles I empeyre so my name,
That I be fals; and if I do that lak,
Do strepe me and put me in a sak,
And in the nexte river do me drenche.

I am a gentil womman and no wenche.   990
Why speke ye thus? But men been evere untrewe,
And wommen have repreve of yow ay newe.
Ye han noon oother contenance, I leeve,
But speke to us of untrust and repreeve.'
     And with that word she saugh wher Damyan
Sat in the bussh, and coughen she bigan,
And with hir finger signes made she
That Damyan sholde climbe upon a tree,
That charged was with fruit, and up he wente.
For verraily he knew al hire entente,   1000
And every signe that she koude make,
Wel bet than Januarie, hir owene make;
For in a lettre she hadde toold him al
Of this matere, how he werchen shal.
And thus I lete him sitte upon the pyrie,
And Januarie and May rominge ful myrie.
     Bright was the day, and blew the firmament;
Phebus hath of gold his stremes doun ysent,
To gladen every flour with his warmnesse.
He was that time in Geminis, as I gesse,   1010
But litel fro his declinacion
Of Cancer, Jovis exaltacion.
And so bifel, that brighte morwe-tide,
That in that gardyn, in the ferther side,
Pluto, that is king of Faierye,
And many a lady in his compaignye,
Folwinge his wyf, the queene Proserpina,
Which that he ravisshed out of Ethna
Whil that she gadered floures in the mede—
In Claudian ye may the stories rede,   1020
How in his grisely carte he hire fette—

This king of Fairye thanne adoun him sette
Upon a bench of turves, fressh and grene,
And right anon thus seyde he to his queene:
   'My wyf,' quod he, 'ther may no wight seye nay;
Th'experience so preveth every day
The tresons whiche that wommen doon to man.
Ten hondred thousand [tales] tellen I kan
Notable of youre untrouthe and brotilnesse.

1030 O Salomon, wys, and richest of richesse,
Fulfild of sapience and of worldly glorie,
Ful worthy been thy wordes to memorie
To every wight that wit and reson kan.
Thus preiseth he yet the bountee of man:
"Amonges a thousand men yet foond I oon,
But of wommen alle foond I noon."
   Thus seith the king that knoweth youre wikkednesse.
And Jhesus, *filius Syrak*, as I gesse,
Ne speketh of yow but seelde reverence.

1040 A wilde fyr and corrupt pestilence
So falle upon youre bodies yet to-night.
Ne se ye nat this honurable knight,
By cause, allas, that he is blind and old,
His owene man shal make him cokewold.
Lo, where he sit, the lechour, in the tree.
Now wol I graunten, of my magestee,
Unto this olde, blinde, worthy knight
That he shal have ayen his eyen sight,
Whan that his wyf wold doon him vileynye.

1050 Thanne shal he knowen al hire harlotrye,
Bothe in repreve of hire and othere mo.'
   'Ye shal?' quod Proserpine, 'Wol ye so?
Now by my moodres sires soule I swere

That I shal yeven hire suffisant answere,
And alle wommen after, for hir sake;
That, though they be in any gilt ytake,
With face boold they shulle hemself excuse,
And bere hem doun that wolden hem accuse.
For lak of answere noon of hem shal dien.
Al hadde man seyn a thing with bothe his yen,　　　1060
Yit shul we wommen visage it hardily,
And wepe, and swere, and chide subtilly,
So that ye men shul been as lewed as gees.

What rekketh me of youre auctoritees?
I woot wel that this Jew, this Salomon,
Foond of us wommen fooles many oon.
But though that he ne foond no good womman,
Yet hath ther founde many another man
Wommen ful trewe, ful goode, and vertuous.
Witnesse on hem that dwelle in Cristes hous;　　　1070
With martirdom they preved hire constance.
The Romain geestes eek make remembrance
Of many a verray, trewe wyf also.
But, sire, ne be nat wrooth, al be it so,
Though that he seyde he foond no good womman,
I prey yow take the sentence of the man;
He mente thus, that in sovereyn bontee
Nis noon but God, but neither he ne she.

Ey, for verray God, that nis but oon,
What make ye so muche of Salomon?　　　1080
What though he made a temple, Goddes hous?
What though he were riche and glorious?
So made he eek a temple of false goddis.
How mighte he do a thing that moore forbode is?
Pardee, as faire as ye his name emplastre,

He was a lecchour and an idolastre,
And in his elde he verray God forsook;
And if that God ne hadde, as seith the book,
Yspared him for his fadres sake, he sholde
1090 Have lost his regne rather than he wolde.
I sette right noght, of al the vileynye
That ye of wommen write, a boterflye.
I am a womman, nedes moot I speke,
Or elles swelle til myn herte breke.
For sithen he seyde that we been jangleresses,
As evere hool I moote brouke my tresses,
I shal nat spare, for no curteisye,
To speke him harm that wolde us vileynye.'
  'Dame,' quod this Pluto, 'be no lenger wrooth;
1100 I yeve it up, but sith I swoor myn ooth
That I wolde graunten him his sighte ageyn,
My word shal stonde, I warne yow certeyn.
I am a king, it sit me noght to lie.'
  'And I,' quod she, 'a queene of Fayerye.
Hir answere shal she have, I undertake.
Lat us namoore wordes heerof make;
For sothe, I wol no lenger yow contrarie.'
  Now lat us turne again to Januarie,
That in the gardyn with his faire May
1110 Singeth ful murier than the papejay,
'Yow love I best, and shal, and oother noon.'
So longe aboute the aleyes is he goon,
Til he was come againes thilke pyrie
Where as this Damyan sitteth ful myrie
An heigh among the fresshe leves grene.
  This fresshe May, that is so bright and sheene,
Gan for to sike, and seyde, 'Allas, my side.

Now sire,' quod she, 'for aught that may bitide,
I moste han of the peres that I see,
Or I moot die, so soore longeth me 1120
To eten of the smale peres grene.
Help, for hir love that is of hevene queene.
I telle yow wel, a womman in my plit
May han to fruit so greet an appetit
That she may dien, but she of it have.'

 'Allas,' quod he, 'that I ne had heer a knave
That koude climbe. Allas, allas,' quod he,
'For I am blind.' 'Ye, sire, no fors,' quod she;
But wolde ye vouche sauf, for Goddes sake,
The pyrie inwith youre armes for to take, 1130
For wel I woot that ye mistruste me,
Thanne sholde I climbe wel ynogh,' quod she,
So I my foot mighte sette upon youre bak.'

 'Certes,' quod he, 'theron shal be no lak,
Mighte I yow helpen with myn herte blood.'
He stoupeth doun, and on his bak she stood,
And caughte hire by a twiste, and up she gooth.
Ladies, I prey yow that ye be nat wrooth;
I kan nat glose, I am a rude man—
And sodeynly anon this Damyan 1140
Gan pullen up the smok, and in he throng.

 And whan that Pluto saugh this grete wrong,
To Januarie he gaf again his sighte,
And made him se as wel as evere he mighte.
And whan that he hadde caught his sighte again,
Ne was ther nevere man of thing so fain,
But on his wif his thoght was everemo.
Up to the tree he caste his eyen two,
And saugh that Damyan his wyf had dressed

73

1150 In swich manere it may nat been expressed,
But if I wolde speke uncurteisly;
And up he yaf a roring and a cry,
As dooth the mooder whan the child shal die:
'Out, help; allas, harrow!' he gan to crye,
'O stronge lady stoore, what dostow?'

　　And she answerde, 'Sire, what eyleth yow?
Have pacience and resoun in youre minde!
I have yow holpe on bothe youre eyen blinde.
Up peril of my soule, I shal nat lien,
1160 As me was taught, to heele with youre eyen,
Was no thing bet, to make yow to see,
Than strugle with a man upon a tree.
God woot, I dide it in ful good entente.'

　　'Strugle,' quod he, 'ye algate in it wente.
God yeve yow bothe on shames deth to dien.'
He swived thee, I saugh it with mine yen,
And elles be I hanged by the hals!'

　　'Thanne is,' quod she, 'my medicine fals;
For certeinly, if that ye mighte se,
1170 Ye wolde nat seyn thise wordes unto me.
Ye han som glimsing, and no parfit sighte.'

　　'I se,' quod he, 'as wel as evere I mighte,
Thonked be God, with bothe mine eyen two,
And by my trouthe, me thoughte he dide thee so.'

　　'Ye maze, maze, goode sire,' quod she;
'This thank have I for I have maad yow see.
Allas,' quod she, 'that evere I was so kinde!'

　　'Now, dame,' quod he, 'lat al passe out of minde.
Com doun, my lief, and if I have missaid,
1180 God helpe me so, as I am yvele apaid.
But, by my fader soule, I wende han seyn

74

How that this Damyan hadde by thee leyn,
And that thy smok hadde leyn upon his brest.'
  'Ye, sire,' quod she, 'ye may wene as yow lest.
But, sire, a man that waketh out of his sleep,
He may nat sodeynly wel taken keep
Upon a thing, ne seen it parfitly,
Til that he be adawed verraily.
Right so a man that longe hath blind ybe,
Ne may nat sodeynly so wel yse,   1190
First whan his sighte is newe come ageyn,
As he that hath a day or two yseyn.
Til that youre sighte ysatled be a while,
Ther may ful many a sighte yow bigile.
Beth war, I prey yow; for, by hevene king,
Ful many a man weneth to seen a thing,
And it is al another than it semeth.
He that misconceyveth, he misdemeth.'
And with that word she leep doun fro the tree.
  This Januarie, who is glad but he?   1200
He kisseth hire, and clippeth hire ful ofte,
And on hire wombe he stroketh hire ful softe,
And to his palays hoom he hath hire lad.
Now, goode men, I pray yow to be glad.
Thus endeth heere my tale of Januarie;
God blesse us, and his mooder Seinte Marie!

Heere is ended the Marchantes Tale of Januarie.

'Ey, Goddes mercy!' seyde oure Hooste tho,
'Now swich a wyf I pray God kepe me fro!
Lo, whiche sleightes and subtilitees
In wommen been. For ay as bisy as bees   121
Been they, us sely men for to deceyve,
And from the soothe evere wol they weyve;
By this Marchauntes tale it preveth weel.
But doutelees, as trewe as any steel
I have a wyf, though that she povre be,
But of hir tonge, a labbing shrewe is she,
And yet she hath an heep of vices mo;
Therof no fors, lat alle swiche thinges go.
But wite ye what? In conseil be it seyd,
Me reweth soore I am unto hire teyd.   122
For, and I sholde rekenen every vice
Which that she hath, ywis I were to nice;
And cause why, it sholde reported be
And toold to hire of somme of this meynee,—
Of whom, it nedeth nat for to declare,
Sin wommen konnen outen swich chaffare;
And eek my wit suffiseth nat therto,
To tellen al, wherfore my tale is do.'

PORTRAIT OF THE MERCHANT
FROM *THE GENERAL PROLOGUE*

A MARCHANT was ther with a forked berd,
In mottelee, and hye on horse he sat;
Upon his heed a Flaundrissh bever hat,
His bootes clasped faire and fetisly.
His resons he spak ful solempnely,
Sowninge alwey th'encrees of his winning.
He wolde the see were kept for any thing
Bitwixe Middelburgh and Orewelle.
Wel koude he in eschaunge sheeldes selle.
This worthy man ful wel his wit bisette:
Ther wiste no wight that he was in dette,
So estatly was he of his governaunce
With his bargaines and with his chevissaunce.
For sothe he was a worthy man with alle,
But, sooth to seyn, I noot how men him calle.

NOTES

1. The first words are an echo of the preceding *Clerk's Tale*, which ends:

   And lat him care, and wepe, and wringe, and waille.

2. *on even and a-morwe* 'night and day'.

10. *at al* 'in every way'.

12. Grisilde is the heroine of *The Clerk's Tale* and symbol of all wifely patience. The complete unreality of the Clerk's narrative wrings a reaction out of the previously dull and taciturn Merchant. He has not been asked to contribute, but his bitter reflexions on the previous tale make him burst out; when he speaks and unloads his story we are prepared for a certain amount of self-identification in the narrative.

14. 'If I were free again, as I hope to thrive.'

15. *the snare* 'marriage'.

18. This is the 'doubting Thomas' and not Thomas of Canterbury. He is said to have evangelized in India. His famous doubt and subsequent capitulation make him especially suitable as a patron saint of affirmation.

19. 'To speak of the majority, though not of all.'

20. *God shilde* 'God forbid'.

22. 'Two months and no more.'

31–2. Here it is evident that he is bursting to speak, to relieve his wounded pride. He claims that he will say nothing more about his own case in his story, but it is easy to read his own cynicism in the tone of the narrative.

33. There are possibly two reasons for the choice of Pavia. Its long standing eminence as a centre for Lombard bankers was in its day matched by its reputation for its brothels, so that it accounts equally for the merchant and his wife.

34. *worthy* 'noble'. This word is much used by Chaucer, but usually in a much less ironic sense. The tale of sensuality that ensues alters our appreciation of Januarie's integrity.

35. We suspect from the word *prosperitee* that the hero is a rich man, and that he is likely to suffer a fall, thus becoming a tragic figure.

38. 'Wherever his appetites led him.' A sharp criticism of his sensuality is contained in these words.

78

39. Scholars have differed over the interpretation of the word
seculeer. In an ecclesiastical context it means a member of the
parish clergy as opposed to a man in regular orders of monks
or friars; it can more simply be interpreted as a layman. Since
the tale in no sense satirizes the Church, which seems to
emerge successfully from it, the second interpretation seems
preferable. Cf. line 110.

41. 'Either for holiness or for senility': a pertinent criticism of
common human motives for religious conversion. Januarie
persists in believing that he is cultivating his soul under the
guise of feeding his bodily lusts.

45. 'To find out a partner who would accept him.'

49–50. The rhyme here *boond/bond* reminds us that the holy
bond of matrimony becomes bondage. It echoes *unbounden* in
line 14 and other images of coupling and snaring in the
Prologue. Immediately we sense the narrator's involvement,
as we do in the heavy sarcasm of these lines.

51–2. Once more the rhyme *bene/clene* gives away a lack of
inner purpose. It is too jaunty and spruce, the content too
familiar, to convey thoroughgoing conviction. The word *esy*
also betrays the speaker. He wants his religion very easily
assumed and dropped. After this every reference to the
speaker's religion is immediately suspect.

53. *paradis* is a most heavily charged word. There is no love-
paradise without a serpent in it somewhere. From this moment
onwards we are looking for the outcome. We want to know how
that outcome will be determined and how it will return to the
legend of the Garden and the Fall.

55. Here opens an extensive digression. Some readers have
seen it as part of the old man's mind working, and it does
follow the line of reasoning which leads him to marry. It may
be the reflexion of the narrator, in which case it is to be taken
as heavily sarcastic. In either case there is irony, because what
is said is so true in the case of a fine and tender marriage and so
false of a man who sees marriage as a commercial transaction
to convey his soul into safekeeping. Quotation marks are not
to be found in medieval manuscripts. Without them it is difficult to apportion the speech to the Merchant or to Januarie.
As here printed they are the words of the narrator.

58. *fruit of his tresor* A careful confusion of images of fertility
and finance. After this it becomes still more clear that he is
buying a wife, seeing her as a new and necessary type of

purchase. He cannot experience the love that is not to be measured in economic terms.

60. The need for an heir is a prime economic factor. (It entered also into *The Clerk's Tale*, as the reason for Walter's marriage.) It enters ironically into the narrative at the climax.

62. The chief 'bacheler', Damyan, has little cause to bemoan his fate at the end of the story, and he leaves *adversitee* for the married man. The suggestion here is that marriage puts an end to the small sorrows of love.

65. *it sit wel* 'it suits well', 'it is most fit'.

67. *brotel ground* Perhaps an allusion to the parable of the house built upon sand.

69. The association of both *brid* and *beest* returns when a gross seduction takes place up among the birds' nests.

71. *ther as* 'whereas'.

72. *ordinaat* 'well ordered', 'secure'.

73. The bond of matrimony has now become a *yok*, which can bind together unwilling partners.

75. The rhetorical question here and another just after are pointers to the development of the irony when it is time to return to these ideas. May later claims that all she is doing is for his health and to assist his recovery.

79. *nis nat* Double negatives used in Chaucer's poetry strengthen the negation and do not cancel it. They also occupy one more syllable for metrical purposes.

80. *til he sterve* 'until he dies' (from any cause).

82. *he Theofraste* 'the famous Theophrastus' (author of *The Golden Book of Marriage*). The two words in grammatical apposition give emphasis. This construction with proper names is found frequently in this Tale. For Theophrastus on Marriage see Appendix in James Winny's edition of *The Wife of Bath's Prologue and Tale* (C.U.P.), pp. 123-5.

83. *What force* 'what matter'.

84. *housbondrye* 'economy'. Economic imagery blends in a pun on the word. It prepares us for the ideas derived from household economy which follow. The other part of the pun is of course a play on the word 'husband'. The Pilgrims have already had such thoughts presented by the Wife of Bath in her Prologue, lines 308-10.

86. Damyan, whom we are later to meet as the third term in this marital triangle, is a servant in this palazzo. From this point the ironies of the tale become too numerous and forceful to be

signposted in the notes. Only the most alert reading will
bring out the care with which Chaucer has worked out fore-
tastes and afterthoughts and made of them a most subtle
blend. Damyan is also the *trewe knave* in line 90, who
'husbands' the master's goods (and wife).

91–2. 'Than a woman who is always waiting to be left your
goods (in your will).'

93–4. This couplet is a problem: different manuscripts have
widely different versions because the poet left it unaccount-
ably incomplete. There is no point in reprinting these con-
jectures since none of them is clearly genuine. They are to be
found in F. N. Robinson's edition of Chaucer to which
readers are referred. The word *hoold* Chaucer is asking us to
save up for the moment of Januarie's blindness when he
clings to his wife in utter desperation.

95. sentence 'opinion', as in *sententia* (Lat.).

101–2. Fortune's gifts are expressed entirely in the terms of
economic inheritance.

107. This passage, reminiscent of the idiom of the medieval
pulpit or *The Parson's Tale*, reveals Chaucer's love of theological rhetoric. He turns to it at all times; here as a prelude
to what is only the parody of a marriage-relationship.

113–17. This passage has affinities with one from the Wife of
Bath whose husband Jankyn told the Genesis story with more
tragic emphasis and greater truth:

> Of Eva first, that for hir wikkednesse
> Was al mankinde broght to wrecchednesse,
> For which that Jhesu Crist himself was slain.   (715–17)

The Merchant is interpreting the thoughts coursing through
Januarie's deluded mind, but Jankyn's interpretation of
Paradise is nearer to Januarie's later experience.

120. The conclusion is lyrical, further and further from the dis-
enchanting reality that awaits the old knight. It leads forward
to the creation of a paradise garden for Januarie and May to
roam in, the place in which *disport* was carried on by the
wrong couple.

121. The ideal wife is *buxom* (obedient), *vertuous*, *ententif*; his
helpe and his *confort*, but May is none of these things. Chaucer
is piling up the qualities in which she is completely lacking.

123. O *flessh* 'one flesh', an allusion to Christ's words on
marriage.

123–4. The rhyme *gesse/distresse* throws the emphasis upon the correct word. The reader should feel the finality of the distress.

130 ff. The comic picture of complete obedience seems to recapture the unrealistic mood of Grisilde's story. It is as if the Wife of Bath had not disposed of such romance for ever. We may sense the scorn of the narrator as he dramatizes and makes of it a complete caricature.

144 ff. In this passage Chaucer makes considerable use of Albertano, *Liber Consolationis* ('The Book of Consolation') and Deschamps, *Miroir de Mariage* (see pp. 26–7). It is now the moment at which any preacher of the period would begin to cite his examples (known as *exempla*) from the Bible to make his point. Four such incidents (characteristically beginning 'Lo', where we would say 'For instance') are now recalled in swift succession.

150–62. This passage is composed of four *exempla* from the Old Testament. While all are said to develop the biblical theme of the Deliverance of the Israelites a note of duplicity is also heard. Rebecca (Genesis xxvi) deceived her blind husband by substituting Jacob for Esau and gaining for the wrong son his father's blessing. Judith saved her people by deceiving and slaying Holofernes (Judith xi–xiii) while Abigail (1 Samuel xxv) saved her husband later to make a marriage-contract with David. Finally, Esther (Esther vii) pleaded the cause of the Israelites and secured the promotion of Mordecai at the expense of the life of Haman. From l. 1052 of the Tale May and the goddess Proserpine unite in the deception of Januarie. By stretching the interpretation a little, the moment when Proserpine inspires her protégée during her crisis of confidence is a deliverance of the fair sex. Thus Chaucer sets up a series of contrasting female figures throughout the Tale.

163. *gree superlatif* 'superior in degree'. This thought has been traced not to Seneca but to Albertano, *op. cit.*

165. This is from Dionysius Cato, *Distichs*.

169. The weeping and wailing of the opening of the Prologue returns. It helps to remind us what an emotional peom this is. Especially the male characters suffer a great deal. This suggests the emotion and the rancour of the narrator who cannot resist the temptation to play upon his audience.

170. 'Where there is no wife to keep house'.

172. Marriage in the Middle Ages was viewed as a human image of Christ's devotion to his Church. Such reflexions gain a cruel ironic emphasis in the present Tale. The Biblical allusions lift the narration intentionally above the reality that too soon grows sour and sordid. The religious assurances offer no joy, they are so frequent and glib.

174. *hateth his flessh* Man and wife are 'one flesh' (see line 123).

182. *inwith his dayes olde* 'in his old age'.

184. *hony-sweete* A palpable exaggeration. Even the least attentive reader must remark that the Merchant is 'laying it on thick'.

187. At this point the narrative is resumed. Januarie starts the speedy search. He has waited too long, and he sends out friends in all directions to comb the neighbourhood for suitable young women. He persists with the dignified reasons for marriage but is treating the process as a furtive purchase.

188. *hoor* 'white-haired'. Cf. line 249.

189. *woot* 'knows'. A great deal of emphasis is to be found upon this verb in the ensuing lines. It serves to remind us that Januarie is totally devoid of self-knowledge, he is still blind to his real condition, and deluded.

   pittes brinke 'the edge of the grave'. Cf. Psalm xxx: 'Thou hast kept me alive. I should not go down to the pit.'

191. *despended* Another spending image, showing unwise 'husbandry'.

198. 'I will have sought out, for my part.'

200–1. 'Since you are many and I one, you will find such a person quicker.'

202. 'Whom it would be best for me to wed.' Unfortunately he has made so great an issue of speed that nobody has time to find a truly suitable wife.

205. The disparity in age is crucial. A medieval man of sixty would be viewed as one of nearly seventy-five today. Cp. the situation in *The Miller's Tale*.

206–10. The images here clinch the position. Pike and bulls are not given to mankind to emulate: they are neither discreet nor temperate creatures. There is a coarse rapacity about the realization that should warn the reader that Januarie has no genuine concern for the state of his soul. *Bene-straw* is another debasing image. It may remind us of the Wife of Bath's confession:

> The flour is goon, there is namoore to telle;
> The bren, as I best kan, now moste I selle.

This is the statement of a middle-aged woman with similarly coarse and rapacious habits.

212. The reference to Wade's boat has never been understood since the Middle Ages. Many references and derivations have been suggested and scholars have grown heated in their wrangles on the interpretation of this phrase. It is derived from a magic boat and here implies skill. *Craft* does not necessarily have a derogatory meaning: it is the craft of sailing.

213. *broken harm* The most recent interpretation of this phrase is 'make use of harmful behaviour when it suits them'.

215. 'To have been to several schools makes clever scholars.'

218. This is the first appearance of one of the reiterated words of this Tale, see line 905.

221. 'If it happened to me to be so unlucky.'

223 ff. The verse here achieves force and pressure from the sharpness of his determination and the strength of the ironies embedded in it. The language is unusually violent: *go streight to the devel, houndes had me eten*. Both the Merchant and Januarie seem to come alive: the feeling of the narrator gives pressure to the poetry.

232. *page* Probably another concealed reference to Damyan, for whom we are kept waiting until the wedding makes an adulterous intrusion possible.

234 ff. This passage seems to criticize the sentiments expressed in *The Parson's Tale*, endorsing St Paul's view that to contract a marriage for the purpose of avoiding sin is justifiable. It will be admitted that it is an essentially negative approach to a way of life that needs positive direction from the Church. The ideal expressed here is sometimes that man and wife should live almost as brother and sister apart from the necessary sexual intercourse 'for the lawful begetting of children to the glory of God'. The language of this passage draws upon such words as *leccherye* but primarily upon more euphemistic expressions: *paramour, dette, leveful procreacioun*. These seem to provide a carpet of snow over the sharper outlines of crisp vital language. Line 244 sharply repudiates this mealy-mouthed attitude; Januarie wants his pleasures.

235. *take him a wyf* 'let him take a wife'.
246. *stark and suffisaunt* 'strong and physically active'.
249 ff. The image of the wintry tree is a compelling one. Januarie mistakes the snow for spring blossom. He admits to having white hair but young green limbs, a position faced earlier by the Reve in his Prologue:

> For in oure wil ther stiketh evere a nail,
> To have a hoor heed and a grene tail.

The Reve shows some self-knowledge, but Januarie only self-delusion. The image, finally, demonstrates visually that Januarie is a figure in contrast to the blossomy season of May, the name of his future wife.

254. The image of *Laurer*, as an evergreen, recurs in the garden scene, line 825.
257–9. This is one of Chaucer's favourite devices: testing public opinion by swiftly changing focus upon individual views until they become a chorus.
263. With the introduction of the two brothers a new episode is brought forward. The name *Placebo* means 'I shall please', while *Justinus* conveys a sense of hard judicious thinking in the negotiations that follow. They act as the Good and Evil Angels and allegorize the two opinions passing through Januarie's own mind.
269–71. 'Except that you are so wise and your nature is so judicious that you do not care to ignore the advice of Solomon' (Ecclesiasticus xxxiii).
273. *by conseil* 'advisedly'.
277. *so wisly* 'so assuredly'. Cf. line 963.
280. *court-man* 'courtier', but also 'flatterer': not so much an adviser as a sycophant.
285. 'I have never disagreed with any of them': a perfect summary of the sycophant's profession. The speaker becomes repetitive, he is falling over himself to prove agreeable as the perfect reflexion of Januarie's own thoughts.
292. 'Should surpass his lord's understanding with his own private opinion.'
301. *heigh corage* 'it is a courageous action'. There is a pun here on the word *corage* meaning sexual potency, the sense in which it is most often employed in this story.
302. *that stapen is in age* 'who is far advanced (stepped) in age'.
303. *by my fader kin* 'by my father's family-tree'.

304. 'Your heart is most conspicuously happy.'

306. His final line throws the whole problem back upon the prospective bridegroom: so that all he has said for nearly fifty lines merely feeds his hearer's prejudices.

311 ff. 'A man ought to consider very carefully the person he gives away his land and his goods to.' Seneca discusses this in *De Beneficiis* I.

324. *mannissh wood* 'crazy for male company'.

326. 'Nobody in the world is satisfactory in all points.' The word *trotteth* suggests an image from horses.

330. 'More good points than vicious ones.'

334. 'Let him who will praise the lot of a married man.'

336. 'And duties, devoid of all happiness.'

339–41. 'They say I have a wife of the utmost integrity, the humblest possible on earth; yet I still know where the shoe pinches.' Justinus adopts the viewpoint we identify with the Merchant rather than Januarie.

342. 'You may, as far as I am concerned, do what you like.'

347–9. 'The youngest man in this present company has his work cut out to keep his wife for himself.' There is raised at once the fear that a young wife will not remain loyal even to a young man. The rest follows logically.

353. *yvele apaid* 'displeased'.

355. *Straw for thy Senek* 'you may keep your Seneca'.

357. *scole-terms* 'scholastic phrases'.

361. 'Who hinders matrimony, certainly.'

364. The consultation is closed and rendered utterly pointless. It has served to give independent voice to the two sides of Januarie's inner debate, but the voice of prudence is snubbed. Self-justification and self-delusion grow throughout the rest of the Tale. We have to decide how we can learn to look at him with sympathy in the stages of courtship and marriage: is he being unfairly treated, or does he deserve everything that follows?

365. A new section opens, with an imaginative projection into Januarie's busy mind: he is a victim of his own *heigh fantasye*—self-delusion—and his *curious bisynesse*, or anxious activity, is self-defeating.

368 ff. This passage is crucial in the development of the story. It offers us the romantic confusion of Januarie's mind, and in the image of the mirror provides us with a symbolic hint of the reality to come. The reflexions are adolescent daydreams of

partners suitable for a young man. The lady finally chosen
answers the external demands of this symbolic passage, but
none of its inner meaning: she is the *fair shap* and *fair visage*,
but nothing further. See also pp. 20–1.

374–6. 'Januarie began in his own mind to consider the girls
who lived nearby. He could not decide which one to fix his
choice on.'

379. 'For her seriousness of demeanour and her graciousness.'

380. *voys* 'fame'.

382. *ernest and game* These two terms frequently appear
together in Chaucer. They point to that borderland between
acceptance and rejection, the ambivalence in so many of
Chaucer's poetical statements. Do we, we are asked, take the
story or the character seriously or satirically?

385. The consultations were only a formality. He has made his
own decision to become his own *auctoritee*, a strong word in
the Middle Ages, where it possessed overtones of the authority
of the Church as well as political or secular power.

386. The traditional blindness of Cupid must be placed within
the orbit of the poem so that the later physical blindness of the
hero can have its full force.

391. *governaunce* (self-control) and *gentillesse* (good-breeding)
are precisely the qualities that May lacks. They are terms of
the greatest importance in Chaucer's writings, full of ethical
and social significance. See *An Introduction to Chaucer*,
p. 188.

392. *wommanly beringe* implies the qualities of loyalty and
chastity and *sadnesse* a complementary seriousness: on both
scores he is totally deceived. His age has brought him no
judgement in matters of human character.

383. *condescended* 'fixed his choice'.

394. *choys* means both 'his process of selection' and 'the lady
of his choice'.

396–8. 'He thought everybody else's opinion was so lamentable
that it was impossible to advance any case against his choice:
this was his mad delusion.'

402–4. 'He would shorten all their labours: there was no longer
any need for them to go backwards and forwards on his
account; he was provided for and could rest in his decision.'
The image of his friends journeying about depicts their
concern for his welfare, cut short before they can amend his
choice and judgement.

409–10. The opinion that prosperity is a sign of divine favour has always been popular among rich merchants. The word *prosperitee* once more prefigures a fall that is inevitably to come.

413. 'Although she was of a humble station.'

416. The association of *ese* and *hoolinesse* reveals the moral insecurity of the hero. By line 431, however, it has become more truly *ese and lust in mariage*, a much more accurate designation.

417. *mighte han hire al* 'he might wholly possess her'. An obvious irony.

420. 'So to arrange that he should not fail in his design.'

428–9. The medieval idea of the Deadly Sins often took the form of a tree with various branches. Chaucer adopts the image in *The Parson's Tale*. At the end of the present Tale we find the full significance of the reference: sin takes place in the branches of a pear tree with the husband in sight.

435. This speculation is especially cruel: he wonders whether if he takes too great a delight in sensual things he might not be forfeiting his heavenly reward. Once more Chaucer pursues the theological implications with a light hand.

440. *Crist eterne on live* 'Christ who lives for ever'.

444. 'Gave a swift retort to his folly.'

450. *right* 'rite' (the final rite, given after the last confession, at which Januarie may have the chance to repent of his marriage as of a sin).

453–5. 'God forbid but that he should often give a married man grace to repent even sooner....' A sardonic comment.

457–8. 'Don't despair but think on this fact: perhaps she may prove your purgatory.' Here is Justinus' candid replacement for the image of *paradis* preferred by Januarie himself. We may quote here the malice of the Wife of Bath towards just such an elderly husband:

> By God, in erthe I was his purgatorie,
> For which I hope his soule be in glorie.

The word is heavily charged with religious sentiment since it was universally believed that the soul might go through a period of punishment in the afterlife to atone for sins on earth. It may be remembered that Dante, whose poetry Chaucer knew well, visited both Purgatory and Paradise after his first visionary trip to the Inferno.

459–60. The image of purgatorial punishment is pursued with a devastating friskiness: *up to hevene skippe*. The future bride may well be God's *meene* and *whippe* (medium of punishment).

462–9. Justinus puts Januarie in his place. He states, as Januarie's fear had implied, the medieval view that even within the bonds of matrimony too great an emphasis upon the carnal element is displeasing to God. But he suggests the counterweight: marriage as a whole is not 'so great felicitee'.

yow shal lette of youre savacion 'shall make you forfeit your salvation'. This statement is offered in a deliberate manner so that the attitude shall be clearly contained in the poem as a whip to beat Januarie when he departs from the ideal of reasonable marital conduct. In line 468 there may be a concealed insult (i.e. 'you are not capable'); certainly the line is ironical.

473–5. The Wife of Bath is most pertinently cited since it is impossible to exclude her recent comments upon matrimonial conduct from an estimate of the 'marriage that is at hand here'. *Litel space* is clearly ironic because she has talked at great length to the Pilgrims.

476. This parting line presents a difficulty. The reference to the Wife of Bath is a direct remark of the Merchant to the company, followed at once by a return to Justinus. It is not possible to place his farewell after line 472 where it belongs, because of the rhyming-scheme. It must remain as a trivial error on the part of the poet, or a little joke, implying that the Wife is well known, even to the characters in a story.

478. 'They have taken their leave of Januarie and everyone else.'

481. *Mayus*, named at last, appears in the masculine form of the month rather than as a female name. It may be noted that towards the end of the story she is known as *fresshe May*.

485–6. The tempo of the narration speeds up. All romantic or decorative considerations are cast aside, and wedlock emerges as a mercantile transaction: *scrit*, *bond* and *feffed* are words from legal conveyancing and feudal land tenure. Nothing is said about her part in the financial transaction; there is no dowry mentioned. She is simply bought ('signed up', we should say).

490. *hooly sacrement* Either matrimony itself or the nuptial communion. It will be noted that religion plays a prominent and not unworthy part in this ceremony. Januarie has no intention of reducing the place of religion in his nuptials;

everything must seem to be well done by the standards of his class.

492. The Biblical references contained in the marriage service. See, however, p. 12.

496. 'Made everything safe and sound enough with holiness.' There is a cynical ring about this.

497 ff. The description of the nuptials is one of the highlights of the poem. It may strike a modern reader as a poetic recreation of the world of the Renaissance rather than of the Middle Ages. The classical deities seem to spring from a Botticelli canvas. As a result, the participants gain through the association. It provides a colourful prelude to the nuptial chamber scene in which there is no cause for continuous rejoicing.

504. Orpheus, the Greek prince, charmed the whole of the natural creation with his lyre; Amphion is alleged to have assisted the building of the walls of Thebes by his control of sound waves.

506. 'At every course of the banquet....'

507. Joab blew a trumpet and stopped a battle (2 Samuel ii).

508. Theodamas is alleged to have encouraged the besieged Thebans with his trumpet calls.

510. Bacchus the wine-god 'pours for them all'.

511–16. Venus has a great deal to laugh about in so old a devotee who had shown his mettle as a bachelor ('in libertee') and now wants to show it as husband. Her torch is the light that heads the procession. Cf. line 566 where the repetition heightens the irony.

518. *Ymeneus* 'Hymen'.

519. 'Had never in his life seen so happy a bridegroom.'

520. *Marcian* is Martianus Capella, author of the poem *The Wedding of Philology and Mercury*. The intensive *hire* and *him* will again be noted.

526. This line recalls the whole poem to its basic theme in folklore, the convention of the old husband and the young wife. From this concise statement Chaucer has elaborated the whole poem.

527. But the mirth has a cutting edge. One sense of this couplet is 'when kindly youth consents to look after declining age, it is a matter for indescribable joy'. Another is 'when the old are foolish enough to marry the young, it is a matter for unspeakable joking'.

532–3. Esther looked meekly upon Ahasuerus when she was plotting the death of Haman (Esther v).

538–42. *ravisshed in a traunce* carries on the mood of his bride-search and shows a similar failure to understand his moral position. The darker side of his self-delusion comes out in the threats (*manace*) of violent love-making. Though he sees himself as Paris it would be truer to recognize in him the cuckolded husband Menelaus. So with a classical reference Chaucer makes a most telling metaphor. Remember also the underlying seasonal metaphor (winter menaces spring, but spring outlasts winter).

543–7. Here it may be thought that he is chattering to keep his spirits up and compensating for his lack of successful action with a spate of impressive words like *corage* and *keene*.

550–2. There are many classical parallels for these sentiments. At a moment of overwhelming tragedy in Marlowe's *Faustus*, there occurs a quotation from Ovid *lente, lente currite, noctis equi* ('run slowly, slowly, horses of the night'). In the present instance Januarie has forfeited sympathy because of his unseemly gloating. The last sentiment which seeks to get rid of the wedding guests is humorously effective.

553–5. 'Finally he does all he can in various cunning ways to force the party to break up without causing offence.' It will be seen, however, that there is a conventional order of doing such things and the guests are not swift to depart.

560. Damyan, the true Paris to May's Helen of Troy, enters early into the marriage to make it a courtly-love triangle. Chaucer may have been well aware that St Damian was a patron of medicine and able to give an ironic undertone to the sight-healing offered as the excuse for the tree-tryst in ll. 1175–6

563. *verray peyne* A conventional expression of the pangs of love which can be paralleled in many other courtly pieces. It will be noted, however, that descriptions of love resort to a violent vocabulary.

564. 'He almost swooned and died in his shoes.' The verb *swelten* also acquires a phallic association.

567. Dispatched to bed, Damyan is now the courtly lover in the throes of the love-emotions often called *hereos*, the violent effects of too great an indulgence in sensual speculation.

571 ff. In this passage Chaucer once more indulges his delight in the device of apostrophe. Passages of sententious writing and moral exhortation are often found in *The Canterbury Tales*.

The intention is to dramatize the emotion to a heroic extent, only to let the tone down when its ignoble qualities are fully revealed.

571. *bedstraw* The straw used for stuffing mattresses. No fire could be more intimately domestic (and by analogy, no betrayal could strike more closely).

573. 'O treacherous and false domestic servant.' *Servant* and *hewe* have the same meaning. The duplication is part of the overdramatization of this paragraph.

574. The moment for the introduction of the serpent image into the marital paradise. The old form *naddre* (adder) is noteworthy.

576. *dronken in plesaunce* 'almost drowned in lusts'.

578. *thy borne man* 'a man born on your estate'.

580. This ironic line prefigures the poem's climax when the blinded Januarie receives his sight back just in time to spy his wife with her lover in the pear tree.

583 ff. A periphrastic way of announcing that the sun is going down, having 'completed his diurnal round'. Chaucer frequently resorts to the conventions of contemporary astronomical literature in order to announce that the time is passing and to herald the arrival of the next event. In all classical and English poems celebrating the ceremony of marriage, the arrival of evening is given due attention, since it heralds the blessing of the bridal bed and the withdrawal of all the visitors.

593-4. Having exhausted the conventional material, Chaucer now comes forward with a camera-eye to catch the unusual preparations of the husband in the next few lines.

595-7. He clearly requires aphrodisiacs to maintain his potency: hippocras, clarified and sweet white wines were used for this purpose. Chaucer dwells upon them as unnatural indulgences.

598-9. Constantine Afer, an eminent doctor of the eleventh century, wrote the book mentioned. He is also one of the medical authorities listed in the *General Prologue*.

605. The drawing of the curtains is a poetic convention in the epithalamium as is the blessing of the bed (line 607).

606. May, for her part, is completely silent. In Boccaccio's version of this story, she has a great deal to explain. Chaucer chose not to use it but to reduce her to a purely symbolic figure. Cf. Introduction, p. 27.

612. The close-ups of chin and neck, the feeble Wantoning, give a crude realism to the episode. It may be noted that medieval carpenters used dogfish-skin like sandpaper so that this image continues the coarse tone, low style and realism.

616 ff. Because he wants to play for time he addresses one of his sermons on marriage to her: she makes no response.

618. *I wil doun descende* 'I will go to sleep'.

623. *no fors* 'no matter'.

626. His sermonizing has now reached the dangerous point: that marriage sanctifies the old lusts which undergo no change in their intensity. In *The Parson's Tale* (line 860) Chaucer reveals a different attitude.

633. There is an attractive side to this: it is a good and natural thing to sing when in love, even though the voice has gone. For a moment there is an image of successful love though it is immediately dashed.

635–6. The animal images add comedy and establish at the same time a completely brutal assessment of life's possibilities, an attitude that was first brought to notice in the images of pike and bulls. See also line 653.

643–4. This brief quotation is his *aube* or dawnsong, appropriate to true lovers in romantic situations. In *The Reve's Tale* (line 4237) is a similar snatch.

654 ff. The technique of narration—in which the speaker seems to be addressing his puppets—adds greatly to the dramatic nature of the contrast as he moves from the completely cold wife to the hot lover.

665. *putte his lyf in aventure* 'endangered his life'. Damyan's reactions at this point are timid and completely devoid of heroism.

669. *compleynt* a poetic lamentation; *lay* a song.

673–5. A complex piece of astronomy used to pass over the gap of time and point to the absurdity of this particular bride's obeying the conventional abstentions. See also appendix on p. 103.

686. Such thoughtfulness towards a servant, though it precipitates a near-tragedy, is a point in Januarie's favour. He takes his position as the master of a household seriously.

692. *Which letted him* 'that prevented him'.

694. *me forthinketh* 'causes me regret'.

697. It is true that he is *secree* but hardly discreet.

699. *manly* This his behaviour does not yet proclaim. The sexual element in this word and also in *servisable* should not be forgotten, since his task seems to be to serve May and get her with child.

709. *At after-mete* 'shortly after dinner'.

712. *Gentil* since he is a man of noble rank though in service upon a greater man.

714. 'After I have just taken a little rest.'

715. *I wole abide* 'I am waiting'.

724. *he say* 'he saw'.

727. *withouten moore* 'without a word of explanation'.

730–1. 'I implore you not to disclose this; I am as good as dead if this should be made known.' Her presence does not elevate his valour.

736. With the rhythm of this line compare lines 611 and 1201. All these create in the verse one characteristic situation: as a lover he is reduced effectually to a fondler and a stroker. He is also a *voyeur* (line 746). These habits do not coincide with genuine sexual ardour and the verse is used to provide this judgement in its movement and sound.

745. A most ingenious interpretation of this line has been given by an American scholar who supports it with a wealth of related instances. Quite clearly *cough* in its modern meaning fits the context perfectly, but it has been shown that it could be read as the bird, the 'chough'. The attractiveness of this lies in the fact that it is a chough that reveals adultery in *The Manciple's Tale* so that a morning call from this bird would be full of symbolic purpose.

746–9. Described in this manner the request is made to appear utterly repulsive. May's reaction is unchanging 'whether she wanted to or not'. A most savage light shines upon his thoughts of theological justification: everything, after all, takes place under the sacred yoke of matrimony. The narrator retires coyly into a corner with the disarming innocence often revealed by Chaucer when he has a passage of comic obscenity to relate.

755–8. 'Whether it were destiny or chance, the power of influences or the natural outcome or the conjunction of the stars in the sky.' There is no precise demarcation between these alternatives.

759. *putte a bille of Venus werkes* 'to start a love-affair'.

764. 'May He judge us all.' Theological speculations come to a halt: the story is now pressing.

770-1. 'I do not mind who is going to dislike this deed.'

773. She has laughed at Januarie in his shirt; now she thinks more tenderly of Damyan in the same attire.

774. What has been called Chaucer's favourite line since it occurs so often. The idea that love ran towards the heart was common in Italian poetry and one that attracted Chaucer, who was often deeply involved in the presentation of emotions. May had none at all from her husband and was obliged to find her emotional life elsewhere. There is, however, little idealism in the treatment of this scheming bride.

775. *excellent franchise* 'noble generosity'.

776. *hem narwe avise* 'take deliberate steps'.

777-82. A conventional passage upon the hard-heartedness of some women towards their lovers presented as an excuse for her consequent action. She has to find outlets for her *pitee*.

780. *grace* 'favour'. This word is in courtly idiom. It is borrowed from the language of divine love and was intended to sanctify what was, as in the present instance, an unhallowed liaison.

793-4. 'She wrung him by the hand warmly but so secretly that nobody noticed.' It is ironic that May is invited by her husband to visit her lover when he is in bed but cannot find any opportunity to join him there.

795. *been al hool* 'recover completely'. A blessing from the lady is bound to do the trick. It is another common phrase in love poetry. Criseyde says the same to Troilus:

Now beth al hool, no lenger ye ne pleyne.

796. Januarie orders his wife as if she were a servant.

799. The cure is sudden and total. 'He combs, preens and adorns himself.'

801-2. 'He presents himself to Januarie and bows as low as a dog crouching for prey.' *Bowe* is from bow and arrow.

806. Another favourite Chaucerian phrase. The Squire in the *General Prologue* has the same phrase: both young men are totally typical as courtly youths of the age. We recall that everything related of Damyan is drawn from this stereotype. The only reason May falls in love with him is that she is *mannissh wood* and her husband is useless to her.

809–10. The Epicurean philosophy suits the arch-sensualist Januarie with his yearning to live *ful deliciously*.

817 ff. This garden with its splendour is an enclosure of beauty and great symbolic import. It is the scene of the Tale's climax and Chaucer is deeply indebted to many medieval traditions in creating it. However, he modifies these traditions himself. Medieval literary gardens never look the same again to the reader when he knows the pear-tree story. See Introduction, pp. 8–16.

820. Guillaume de Loris devised the idealized and allegorical garden mentioned.

822–3. 'Neither would the power of Priapus enable him to tell, though he is god of gardens.' It should be added that he is also the priapic god, a god of sex. Normally Venus the goddess of more mystical love-making would have been introduced at this point in a conventional love-vision.

826–7. Pluto, the dark god of the underworld, was often confused with Plutus the god of riches. He therefore has several affinities with Januarie the merchant. Proserpina is presented with all her fairies, although they properly belong to a different mythology. It should be noted that she is a militant feminist in the narrative. Traditionally she spends six months of the year away from her dark and sordid husband.

831–2. 'Had such an overwhelming pleasure in walking and taking exercise in it that he would let no one else have the key.'

833–4. The rhyme *wiket/cliket* is the most powerful provided in the text. It is onomatopoeic. Each time it is used it marks a stage in the steady development of the poem's climax. A *cliket* is to become a symbol of male domination: whoever has the key to the gate has the right to the lady within the garden. It may also be seen as the key to a cashbox, and a final revelation of the mercenariness of this marriage. The association of a love garden with an aged lecher and a scheming woman destroys the expected charm of the place and the atmosphere *in somer seson*. Surely all this must come to a stop, we demand.

836. *paye his wyf hir dette* is a euphemism. See also line 240. It is appropriate in the general context of mercenariness.

846. The scorpion may well be the sign of the zodiac, Scorpio. See appendix on p. 103.

849. *brotil* We recall the word from line 67 where it occurs twice. 'O brittle joy, subtly deceiving poison'

852. *moore and lesse* 'great and small'.

855–6. 'Now hast thou deprived him of the use of his two eyes, the misery of which has caused him to seek for death.' Like Gloucester in *King Lear*, Januarie has not shown moral vision while his eyes were sound.

857. *free* For a comment on this word see *An Introduction to Chaucer*, p. 188.

858. *lust and prosperitee* There have been many such couplings of abstract terms in this narrative. This one is sharp and critical, showing how short-lived his true prosperity is.

860. Cf. line 1.

865–8. 'He did not wish her to be loved or married in his life-time or afterwards but to live perpetually in widow's black, alone like the turtle-dove which has lost her partner.'

871. *noon oother* 'not otherwise'.

873–4. 'He could not stop being consumed by jealousy.'

878. *go* here means 'walk'.

879. This departure in the story poses a dilemma. How can she elude his grasp which afflicts her all day as well as all night? He is trying to mould all her behaviour as *warm wex* in his hands; the crucial symbol of line 905 is prefigured. It is Januarie's precise way of demonstrating what he means by their being *o flessh*.

882–3. Januarie has partly recovered from the emotional shock of blindness which left him ready to die. It is now May's turn to express passionate emotion: 'Either she must have the man she has set all her desires upon or she must otherwise die.'

884. *whan* 'until'; *wolde* 'should'.

890. 'Without Januarie hearing it.'

895–6. 'What good would it do you to see as far as the distant horizon?'

897–8. The moral is clear: it is as good to be completely blind as to be deceived when you can still see normally.

899–901. In spite of a hundred eyes Argus was tricked by Zeus in pursuit of Io.

901–3. 'Yet he was blind too, and so are others who think this is not so. It is comforting to be able to pass things over. I have nothing more to say.'

905. *Warm wex*, associated here with the *cliket/wiket* rhyme, acquires still greater depth as a symbol of waywardness in woman.

914–15. 'What cunning plan will not be found out in the pursuit of Love, no matter how long or difficult it may be?'

916–19. The story of Pyramus and Thisbe, told by Ovid in *Metamorphoses* IV, and shorn of the comic associations it is given in *A Midsummer Night's Dream*, is a good example of love's difficulties. Chaucer had already told this story in his 'Legend of Thisbe' part of *Legend of Good Women*.

920–1. The date established in a roundabout manner is 8 June. Astronomical facts are often delivered by Chaucer in a pedantic manner. See also appendix on p. 103.

923. 'Through his wife's urgent pushing.' We are asked to recall how Eve egged on her husband and brought about the primeval catastrophe in the Garden of Eden.

926–36. This passage is a daring parody of The Song of Solomon wrenched out of its Biblical context. There are other overtones in this speech. The dove-images are Biblical, but recall also the doves of Venus. The whole suggests also the scene of the apocryphal story of Susanna and the Elders. For comment on this complex speech see pp. 13–14.

937. *olde lewed wordes* A highly disrespectful comment upon the Old Testament.

938. May, who still keeps silent, reacts to her husband's exhortation with a familiar sign to her lover.

945. *and no wight mo* The narrator enjoys the preparations for the dramatic climax.

947. The sound of the line perfectly echoes the meaning.

950. The Lord sits in heaven above but Damyan will soon be high in the pear tree.

954. Januarie has always seen May as a purchase and not an advantageous investment: he is cleared of the charge of *coveitise*.

957. 'Be true to me' (imperative). The line engages a degree of sympathy in the reader: old age in itself demands respect. It cannot be said that Chaucer has loaded all the dice against his central character.

960 ff. He talks of covenants and charters, prefacing the sexual encounter, in which he is not involved, by another sermon.

963. *wisly* 'truly'.

976–94. After all this time May speaks and echoes the religious sentiments with which she has grown familiar in her year of marriage.

979. *in youre hond* She touches on the sore point of her total lack of freedom.

988. Drowning in a sack was formerly an oriental punishment. Chaucer arranges for her to escape this fate.

992. 'Women get nothing but reproaches from you men all the time.'

998. The pear tree is at last presented. It was part of the old story and the original audience was waiting to see if there would be any new twist in the interpretation of the legend. Three characters are present and all are in a state of antici- patory excitement.

1007–12. Summertime is realized for the reader in the manner of an illuminated manuscript rendered in verse. The position of the sun and the signs of the zodiac are part of the pictorial convention. *Exaltacion*, the moment of greatest influence; *declinacion*, the moment of least influence when a star is going down.

1013–1107. This prolonged debate between two deities acts as a completely original viewpoint for the narrative. Having come down to earth after the passage of astronomical learning, we are conveyed below ground for the next change of focus. In one of Chaucer's sources St Peter is the intervening authority: to employ a god himself uneasily married to a wife who leaves him from February to September is a masterstroke.

1018. According to legend Pluto abducted Proserpina from Sicily, a point noted by Milton in *Paradise Lost*, Book IV, and corrected in some later MSS of *The Merchant's Tale* to the corruption of the text.

1020. On the importance of Claudian's version of the legend, see Introduction, pp. 28–9.

1028. A word is missing from MS versions: *tales* and *stories* have been added to modern editions as being the obvious interpretation.

1030. It is notable that Pluto, the god of the underworld and of money, who takes the unhappy Januarie under his pro- tection, has Biblical allusions at the ready. He is attractively presented as a man full of worldly wisdom and a sane disbelief in feminine pretensions: a very human god.

1033. 'To every man who has sufficient brain and common- sense.'

1038. Jesus the author of Ecclesiasticus is meant, and not Jesus Christ. Although Pluto selects only the passages which are irreverent towards women, this does not represent Jesus' entire opinion.

1045. One of Chaucer's finest comic lines, having both the visual and auditory quality to bring the scene indelibly to the mind.

1047. The adjective *worthy* is spoken without irony or malice by this witness.

1051. 'To the shame of herself and her whole sex.'

1052. '"Oh will you?" said Proserpina, "so that's what you want?"' Of lines 1052–98 it may be remarked that Chaucer seems to enjoy giving long, angry, incoherent and slightly illogical speeches to his female characters. Cf. May's speech above.

1053. Saturn was her grandfather. His powers as a god were exercised in the creation of discord and evil.

1058. 'Face up to their accusers.' The *suffisant answere* that Proserpina is now preparing was a traditional part of this fable. Here it is suggested as a boon for the entire sex and a permanent challenge to their accusers. See also note to lines 150–62.

1060–1. 'Although a man had seen it happening with his two eyes, yet a woman will be able to brazen it out.'

1063. *lewed as gees* 'ignorant', 'silly as geese'.

1064. 'What do I care for all your [Biblical] authorities?'

1066. 'Found many of us women fools' (fools enough to marry him, presumably).

1070 ff. This is the moment when Chaucer marshals Biblical stories as examples of his interpretation of human behaviour. Here he offers a brief passage: the sources are the writings of Albertano, Deschamps and St Jerome.

1071. St Cecilia the martyr, the subject of *The Second Nun's Tale*, is meant.

1072–3. The Roman examples are headed by Lucretia, the victim of the sadistic Tarquin.

1076. 'I beg you to understand the real gist of his remark.'

1077–8. 'Nobody but God is supremely good: neither man nor woman.'

1083. There is a special humour for the more learned participants in the pilgrimage in hearing two 'false gods' discussing Solomon's delight in strange deities.

1085. 'however you try to whitewash him': a commonsense debating-point.

1088–90. She refers to I Kings xi.

1090. *rather than he wolde* 'sooner than he wished to'.

1096. 'As certainly as I hope to retain my tresses of hair.'

1098. 'To speak evil of him that means us harm.'

1099. Pluto is perhaps a little alarmed at the storm he has raised, and the torrent of reproach.

1103. 'I am a king, it does not become me to break my word.'

1108. For the last time the focus of the poem changes, showing Januarie at a pitch of lyrical, happy 'fantasye'.

1113–14. *pyrie/myrie* Another of the jaunty menacing rhymes that operate upon the reader as sound-images of significance in themselves. Chaucer is not always as skilful with his rhymes as he is in this Tale, but here he controls the rhetoric of rhyme as skilfully as Alexander Pope was to do.

1117 ff. May's subterfuge is to pretend to a violent longing for what is dangling down from the tree. Her sudden aching is attributed to an early stage in pregnancy (*my plit*). In comedy, a pregnant woman often expresses crazy longings for unsuitable foodstuffs. Januarie is of course enraptured that an heir may be in the offing and is happy to assist her into her lover's arms—from which she is more likely to emerge pregnant in due course. *Fruit* in line 1124 reminds the reader of the tree in Eden.

1130. He is to embrace the tree largely to prevent anybody else from following her up: this is the only explanation of the following remark.

1136. She is treading on him physically and metaphorically on her way to Damyan's arms. We imagine him embracing the tree he has himself offered as a symbol of sexuality:

> I fare as dooth a tree,
> That blosmeth er that fruit ywoxen bee. (249–50)

1139. *I am a rude man* Chaucer pretends coyness in the face of an erotic incident. He repeats the same disingenuousness at lines 1150–1 and near the conclusion of the *General Prologue*.

1141. The suddenness of this action disposes of any tenderness in this relationship. It is as coarsely physical as Januarie's love-making, although more pleasant to May. He thrusts himself upon her, difficult as this is to imagine in a pear tree. This line seems to preclude any sympathy for either partner and the preliminary descriptions of their heightened emotions come to nothing when they are finally together.

1146. 'There never was a man so desirous of anything.'

1149. *dressed* 'served', and, of course, 'undressed'.

1151. *uncurteisly* 'in a low manner'.

1153. A reference to the judgement of Solomon?

1155. 'Oh, great impudent lady, what are you doing?'

1159–62. 'On peril of my soul, I am telling the truth. I was
told that there was nothing better to cure your sight than to
struggle with a man up in a tree.' Proserpina inspired this
masterly stroke of impudence.

1165. *on shames death* 'a shameful death'.

1169. 'Truly, if you had really seen.'

1171. *glimsing* 'blurred vision'. She convinces him out of the
evidence of his recovered sense of sight.

1175–6. 'You're all wrong, sir; is this all the thanks I get for the
recovery of your eyesight?'

1177. *kinde* (i) 'generous'; (ii) 'natural in action'—especially
ironic. See *An Introduction to Chaucer*, p. 189.

1181. *I wende han seyn* 'I thought I had seen'.

1188–91. 'Until he has accustomed himself to seeing again.
Naturally a man who has been blind a long time cannot see
well the moment his sight returns.'

1193. *ysatled* 'settled down'.

1194. This seems to threaten a repetition.

1198. 'He who misunderstands comes to a wrong conclusion'—
a proverb.

1201. The rhythm returns to the lulling, caressing movement of
his other lines of love-making. His happiness is an example of
what Swift called 'a perpetual possession of being well
deceived'.

1202. Any offspring that may be expected will probably be
Damyan's. We realize that Januarie will accept the child as his
own, will ask no questions, and will see the provision of an heir
as of paramount importance.

1205–6. *Januarie/Marie* A dramatic rhyme.

1208. Harry Bailly is ready for another of his fatuous inter-
ventions.

1211. *sely men* 'poor men'.

1212. 'They will always depart from the truth.'

1216. *labbing shrewe* 'tittle-tattling wretch'.

1219. 'Do you know what? I'll tell you this in secret.'

1220. *me reweth soore* 'I am very sorry'.

1223. *cause why* A vulgarism still to be found in conversation.

1224. *somme of this meynee* 'somebody in this group' (presumably the Wife).

1226. 'Since women know how to talk on these matters.'

1227. 'And my wits are too weak for that.'

APPENDIX

ASTRONOMICAL INFLUENCES

Chaucer's familiarity with the findings of contemporary astronomy has long been admired. While the present Tale offers him freedom to produce a celestial source for the follies of the human actors he treats this superstructure with such reserve as to allow us to ignore it altogether. In this respect it is quite different from the substructure of Pluto and Proserpina which may be said to enliven the climax of the poem while the comment on human behaviour is similar. The celestial commentary may be detected at three points in the Tale, though proof sufficient for those entirely resistant to such interpretations may be found inadequate.

The marriage of the Knight January with the young Venus May, may recall to the reader of Chaucer the conjunction of Mars and Venus that presided over the nativity of the Wife of Bath and with similar portent. In lines 673–5 of *Merchant's Tale* the wedding is shown to have been celebrated when the moon was in two degrees of the sign Taurus. This has been calculated as implying the conjunction of Mars and Venus. Further investigation of this subject in the articles cited below yields a date for this marriage as 25 March (Lady Day) 1392, while it has also been demonstrated that Chaucer's use of astronomical data very often refers to the year in which the poem was being written. If that is the case here, we have the date of the given Tale.

A stage in the decline of January's fortune is reached in line 846 where the 'scorpion' may well be the sign of the zodiac, Scorpio, which is in the house of Mars – and in this case (as in line 847) stings January with blindness. In such a state he comes, on 8 June, into his garden for the breakdown of his ill-fated marriage and the fate predestined from the conjunction of planets of 25 March. A full but difficult discussion of the astronomical literature is to be found in three articles by J. D. North in *Review of English Studies* 1969

GLOSSARY

abedde in bed
abiden dwell
abregen shorten
adawen recover
again, againes again; against
agasten terrify
ago (inf. *wenden*) gone
al (l. 1060) although
alderfirst first of all
aleye alley
algate wholly
allegen cite; adduce
altercacioun difference
apayen satisfy
apointen determine
appreven approve
ark arc of circle
arreest restraint
arwe arrow
ascencioun rising
assayen prove
assenten agree
assoilen explain
Assuere Ahasuerus
aswagen lessen
attemprely in moderation
avaunt boast
aventure danger; chance
avisement consideration
avisen consider
avoutrye adultery
axen ask
ay (l. 91) all the time
ayen again
bar (inf *bereu*) bore
beden offer
bedrede bedridden
bely-naked completely naked

bene bean, worthless thing
benedicitee bless us (pr. *bencité*)
bene-straw bean straw
beningnely graciously
beningnitee graciousness
benison blessing
beren bear
beringe bearing
bet better
beth (inf. *ben*) be
bifil it happened
bigilen deceive
bille letter; (l. 759) end
biraft (inf. *bireven*) deprived
bit (inf. *bidden*) bids
biwreyen reveal
blent blind
blosmen blossom
bontee excellence, virtue
boone request
borwen borrow
boterflye butterfly
breden breed
bren bran
brennen burn
brere briar
bresten break
brid bird
brotel insecure
brouken keep
buxom obedient
carf (inf. *kerven*) carve
catel goods
Catoun Cato
chaast chaste
chaffare matter, subject
chargen load

chartre document

chees (inf. *chesen*) chose

cherissen cherish

chiden reproach

chidestere reproacher

clarree sweet wine

clerke educated man

cliket key

clippen embrace

cloute fragment

cokewold cuckold, deceived husband

coltissh colt-like, energetic

columbin dove-like, pure

commune common property

compleynt poem of reproach

condescenden decide upon

conseil advice; (l. 1219) secret

constellacion influence of the stars

contrarien oppose

corage courage; (l. 547) sexual ardour

corsen curse

countrefeten duplicate

craft skill

craken croak

crouchen bless with the sign of the cross

curious careful

curteisye courtly, noble behaviour

dar (inf. *durren*) dared

daun dominus, academic title of B.A.

dawen dawn; see clearly

debaat conflict of opinion

deceivable deceptive

declinacion declination (astron.)

deffien defy

delicat delightful, delicious

demen judge

descriven describe

despenden spend

dette debt

devisen imagine

deyntee delight

deyntevous dainty

deys dais, platform

discrecioun discernment

discreet tactful

dispeiren despair

dispense expenditure

disport pleasure

disputisoun disputation

diurne daily

diverse different

dooth (inf. *doon*) do (imper.)

dostow? do you?

doten become senile

doutelees without doubt

dowve dove

dreden doubt

drenchen drown

dressen prepare, make ready

dronkelewe alcoholic

duren endure

eek also

eft again

elde old age

empeyren injure

emplastren bedaub

emprenten imprint

encombraunce hampering

engendren beget

enhauncen exalt

ensample instance

entenden attend

entente intention

ententif devoted, attentive

envenyminge poisoning

er before

eschu averse

eschuen avoid
espien inquire
estaat calling, social estate
esy comfortable
everychon everyone
everydeel in every part
exaltacion rising (astron.)
eylen be ill
fader father
fain gladly, willingly
famulier affable
fantasye delusion
feffen enfeoff, endow
fetten fetch
feynen pretend
fin end
flekked spotted
folily foolishly
folwen follow
fonde, foond (inf. *finden*) found
forage cattle fodder
forberen endure
forgoon (inf. *forgon*) forgo
fors, no of no importance
forthinken cause regret
forward foremost
foule horribly
franchise generosity
ful very
fulfilled filled with
fyrbrond torch
gaderen gather
game fun
gan (inf. *ginnen*) auxiliary
    verb in past tenses
gees geese
geeste tale
gentillesse courtesy (see
    Introduction to Chaucer,
    p. 188)
gladen make glad
gliden pass over

glimsing impaired vision
glosen gloss over
good (n.) goods
governaunce self-control
grace favour
gree degree, rank
grisely terrifying
gyen direct
habounden abound
hals neck
han (inf. *haven*) have
hardily certainly; boldly
harlotrie wickedness
hastif hasty
hemisperie hemisphere
heng (inf. *hangen*) hung
hertely gladly
hewe servant; (l. 852) colour,
    guise
highte (inf. *heten*) is called
hire her; (l. 402) their
homicide murderer
hool in good health
hoold keeping
hoomly domestic
hoor white-haired
houndfissh dogfish
housbondrie economy
iape trick
idolastre idolater
ilke same
instaunce request
inwith in
jalousie jealousy
jangleresse female gossip
japen play a trick
japerye buffoonery
jargon chatter
kan (inf. *konnen*) can;
    (l. 456) know
keep heed
kemben comb

kid (inf. *kithen*) made known

kinde (l. 1177) generous (see
   Introduction to Chaucer,
   p. 189)

knave manservant

konnen be able to; know how to

koude (inf. *konnen*) could

labbing gossiping

labour (l. 650) labourer

laurer laurel tree

lay song, poem

leccherye lust

lechour lustful person

leere (inf. *leren*) learn

leeve believe

lesten please

leten hinder, prevent;
   (l. 1005) allow

letuarie electuary, remedy

leveful lawful

levere rather

lewed ignorant

leyser leisure

lief glad; (l. 1179) love

list it pleases

listen like to

lite little

lives alive

longen belong

looth unwilling

lust inclination

lusty happy

make partner, mate

manacen threaten

marchal master of ceremonies

Mardochee Mordecai

matiere matter

maystow? may you?

mazen be stunned

meene instrument

meschief trouble

mete food

meynee company, gathering

misdemen misjudge

missayen speak amiss

mo more

moebles furniture

moot must (*also moot I thee*,
   as I hope to thrive)

morwe morning

moste must, be obliged

motif argument

mowen may

muchel much

murye merry

naddre adder

namely especially

namoore no more

nas was not

nathelees nevertheless

ne not; nor

nice foolish

nis is not

nolde would not

o (l. 123) one

offenden offer violence to

Olofernus Holofernes

oon one

ootherweys otherwise

ordinaat precisely ordered

orison prayer

orisonte horizon

outen utter aloud

outher otherwise

overal in every way

overmacchen outdo

pace (inf. *passen*) pass

palays, paleys palace, palazzo

panyer basket

papejay parrot

paramour sexual intercourse

paraunter perhaps

paraventure perchance

pardee by God, truly

parfite perfect

parfournen perform

parten diminish

passen surpass

pees peace

penner writing case

pere pear

pestilence plague

peyne suffering

piken adorn

pilwe pillow

pitee compassion

pitte grave

plesaunce delight, lust

pleyen amuse

plit condition

pouren gaze

povre poor

precious (l. 135) fastidious

preven prove

preynen trim

preysen appraise

prime nine a.m.

privee closet

prively secretly

procreacioun reproduction

prudence judiciousness

pryen peer

purtreyen sketch

pye magpie

pyk pike

pykerel young pike

pyrie pear tree

queynte strange

quod (inf. *quethen*) said

ragerye passion

reden counsel

reed advice

rehercen repeat

rekken pay attention to

rennen run

~blyen make objection to

repreven reproach

revel merrymaking

rewen take pity

right so (l. 1189) just so

riven cut

route group

routhe pity

rownen whisper

sad serious

sadnesse seriousness

sapience wisdom

saugh (inf. *seen*) saw

savacion salvation

say (inf. *seen*) saw

scole school

scrit writ

seculeer secular (see note, to l. 39, p. 79)

seelde rarely

sely good, simple, innocent

semblable like, similar

sentence opinion

servisable of service

seyn (inf. *seen*) seen

seyn since

shaltow shall you

shap figure

shapen arrange, contrive

sheene shining

shent (inf. *shenden*) ruined

shilden forbid

shinken pour

shoop (inf. *shapen*) arranged

shrewe ill-tempered woman

shullen shall

sike sick

siken sigh

siker sure, secure

sith, sithen since

sitten suit

skile cause

sleighte trick

slow (inf. *sleen*) slew
solas delight
someres summer's
soothly truly
sop piece of bread
sotile subtle
soul (l. 868) sole
sovereyn supreme
speden prosper
spot harm
standen stand
stapen advance
stark strong
sterten start
sterven die
stidefastnesse integrity
stonden (inf. *standen*) stood
stoore strong
streite strict, narrow
strepen strip
streynen press, force
suffisaunt equal to
suffisen be satisfactory
swelten die
swich such
swinken work
swiven seduce
swownen swoon
taryen delay
terrestre earthly
Tesbee Thisbe
teyd tied, bound
than then
thee (inf. *theen*) thrive,
  prosper
thenken consider
thewes manners
thilke that
tho then
throng (inf. *thresten*) thrust
travers curtain
trespacen trespass, do wrong to

tretee agreement
trompen blow a trumpet
trowen believe
tweye two
twiste twig
unlikly displeasing
unshetten unlock
unstable changeable
usage custom
vanitee illusion
venym venom
vernage sweet white wine
verray true
vileynye bad behaviour (see
  Introduction to Chaucer,
  p. 190)
visagen disguise
vitaille food
voiden empty
vois fame
vouche sauf grant
waden get into difficulties
wan (inf. *winnen*) won
wantown unruly
wele happiness
wenche common woman
wenen imagine
werchen work
wex wax
weyven turn aside from
whan when; (l. 884) until
whilom once
widwe widow
wiflees wifeless
wight man
wiket gate
wirchen work
wise manner
wisly prudently; certainly
wit knowledge; reason (see
  Introduction to Chaucer,
  p. 190)

Glossary

witen doubt; know
wombe stomach
wood mad
woot (inf. *witen*) knows
woxen (inf. *wexen*) become
wrooth angry
yaf (inf. *yeven*) gave
ybroght (inf. *bringen*) brought
ye you; (l. 532) eye
yelden yield, pay
yen eyes
yeven give
yheeren (inf. *heren*) heard
yifte gift

Ymeneus Hymen, god of marriage
ynogh enough
yok yoke; bondage
yoore long ago
ypocras hippocras, a cordial
ysatled (inf. *setlen*) settled down
yse (inf. *seen*) seen
yvele evil
ywis surely
ywoxen (inf. *wexen*) grown
ywroght (inf. *werchen*) made, created